THOMAS COOK
Travellers

KU-215-020

CRETE

BY
CHRISTOPHER CATLING

Produced by AA Publishing

Written by Christopher Catling
Original photography by Philip Enticknap and
Ken Paterson

Edited, designed and produced by AA Publishing.
© The Automobile Association 1996.
Maps © The Automobile Association 1996.

Distributed in the United Kingdom by AA Publishing, Norfolk
House, Priestley Road, Basingstoke, Hampshire RG24 9NY.

Published by AA Publishing (a trading name of Automobile Association
Developments Limited, whose registered office is Norfolk House,
Priestley Road, Basingstoke, Hampshire RG24 9NY. Registered number
1878835) and the Thomas Cook Group Ltd.

Colour separation: BTB Colour Reproduction, Whitchurch, Hampshire.

Printed by Edicoes ASA, Oporto, Portugal.

Cover picture: *the harbour at Iráklio*
Title page: *the Procession Fresco, Knosós*
Above: *one way of getting about the island*

Contents

About this Book

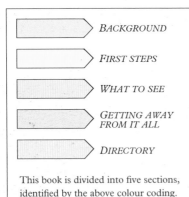

BACKGROUND

FIRST STEPS

WHAT TO SEE

GETTING AWAY
FROM IT ALL

DIRECTORY

This book is divided into five sections,
identified by the above colour coding.

Background gives an introduction to
the country – its history, geography,
politics, culture.

First Steps offers practical advice on
arriving and getting around.

What to See is an alphabetical listing of
the places to visit, interspersed with
walks and tours.

Getting Away From it All highlights
places off the beaten track where it's
possible to relax and enjoy peace and
quiet.

Finally, the **Directory** provides
practical information – from shopping
and entertainment to children and sport.
Special highly illustrated features on
specific aspects of the country appear
throughout the book.

Mirtía, birthplace of the Cretan novelist,
Níkos Kazantzákis

BACKGROUND

'Crete is an island set in the
wine-dark sea,
Fair and fertile, washed by the waves.'
HOMER
The Illiad

Introduction

*B*eauty, fertility and the ever-present sea – the aspects of Crete that Homer singled out for mention in the 8th century BC – are still the principal reasons why people come to Crete today. The sea gently laps the golden sands that stretch endlessly along the island's northern shores. The southern coast, by contrast, is broken into a series of smaller coves, many of them remote from any road, but perfect for creating your own private slice of paradise – as many German hippies did in the 1970s.

Crete's beauty and fertility are features that strike even the most botanically ignorant of visitors if they happen to arrive in spring when the fields, orchards and wayside verges turn into carpets of vividly coloured flowers. That same fertility was the source of the wealth that gave rise to the great Minoan civilisation, which dominated the Aegean from about 2600BC until some mysterious and unknown calamity caused its destruction around 1450BC.

Today, the Minoan palace complex at Knosós, just outside Iráklio, is the island's biggest tourist attraction, though it is just one of hundreds of sites scattered across the island representing the legacy of Minoan, Roman, Venetian and Turkish rule. In addition to this, there are some 600 churches and monasteries, many of them decorated with the fragments of ancient frescos, underlining the island's Byzantine heritage.

CRETE

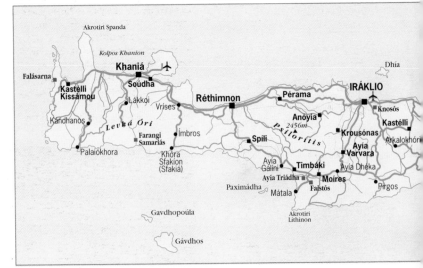

Exploring Crete

Many visitors come to Crete for its beaches and end up hooked on the island's culture, enjoying the adventure of tracking down a Minoan hilltop sanctuary, or its Christian equivalent, a tiny 12th-century church full of serene icons and wall paintings. Such explorations will take you deeper and deeper into the Cretan countryside, where the majesty of the mountain landscapes and the rhythms of the ordinary life of Crete, well away from the tourist haunts and bustling streets of the provincial capitals, will work their magic.

Nowhere is that magic more in evidence than in the simple cafés and tavernas of Crete. Choose one in a quiet fishing village and watch the sun go down as you savour the simple local food and wine while listening to the gentle wash of the waves, accompanied by the song of the cicadas. As you relax in the balmy

COUNTRY LOCATOR

warmth of the evening air, a waiter will appear at your elbow with a dish of fruit or a glass of homemade *raki*, a simple gift from the taverna owner who may later wander over and chat in broken English about his hopes for his grandchildren or his memories of the past. The instinctive warmth of the Cretan character simply adds another dimension to the experience of travelling on this richly varied and rewarding island, known appropriately enough to the rest of Greece as *Megalonissos* – the Big Island.

Byzantine churches are a major feature of the Cretan landscape

Geography

Crete is the largest of the hundreds of islands making up the Grecian archipelago, ranking fifth in the Mediterranean (just behind Sicily, Sardinia, Cyprus and Corsica). The island measures 250km from east to west, but from north to south it is only 60km at its widest and a mere 12km in places.

Crete is also the southernmost point of any significance in Europe (only Gávdhos – see page 119 – is further south). From Crete to the northern coast of Africa it is only 300km across the Sea of Libya, and Crete lies nearer to the equator than both Tunis and Algiers.

Mountains and caves

Distances on Crete are greatly magnified by the mountain ranges that run like a spine down the centre of the island, acting as a barrier to north–south travel. The southern part of the island has always been more remote and less populated than the north, though this is changing as the little fishing villages of the south are discovered by tourists looking for a quiet base.

Crete's mountains are a continuation of the same chain that sweeps down from the Peloponnese, surfacing again on the islands of Karpathos and Rhodes. They are composed principally of limestone which has been eroded into the spectacular gorges and caves for which Crete is famous.

It was in one of these caves (the Dhíktaen – see page 70) that Zeus, destined to rule over the ancient gods, was born. The story of Zeus is perhaps a mythic throwback to the origin of human life on Crete, since many of the island's caves have revealed extensive evidence of neolithic occupation.

Typical Cretan scrub, full of tough but fragrant flowering plants

Vegetation

The name of the Ídhaean cave (see page 100) preserves another memory of the old Crete: *idha* means forest in Doric Greek, and Herodotus, the 5th-century BC Greek historian, refers to Crete as being covered in trees. The island was still well-wooded when the Venetians arrived in the 13th century, but their voracious appetite for ship-building timber, combined with an extensive building programme, began the steady erosion of the indigenous vegetation. Today, only small patches of the original forest survive, consisting of cypress, Calabrian pine and evergreen holm oak, with plane, sweet chestnut and introduced eucalyptus in the river valleys. Taking their cue from the island's ancient forest mix, road builders have planted many new trees to create attractive groves along the verges of the national highway.

The *phrygana*

Those areas of Crete that are not under cultivation are covered in a characteristic scrub called the *phrygana*, the Cretan equivalent to the *maquis* that covers many parts of the Mediterranean. This fragrant mass of wild plants includes many shrubs that are resistant to the island's sheep and goats. Prickly kermes oak and bitter tasting euphorbias cover the hillsides in dense billowing mounds of green, with other plants sheltering in and amongst them to take advantage of their protection. These include herbs such as oregano, sage and thyme, shrubs such as phlomis and cistus, and the wonderful range of wildflowers, bulbs and orchids for which Crete is renowned.

Wildlife

The *phrygana* was once home to the splendidly horned Cretan ibex, or *krí-krí*,

Mountain ranges, once wooded, form the island's central spine

depicted in Minoan art (see, for example, the Peak Sanctuary Rhyton in Iráklio's Archaeological Museum – page 32). Walkers on Crete frequently claim to have seen this shy and elusive animal, but they are now virtually extinct on Crete, surviving only in special offshore nature reserves, such as Ayíi Pántes (see page 75). You are quite likely to spot harmless basking snakes, geckos and wall lizards, and even the occasional chameleon, for though this reptile is a master of camouflage, it gives its presence away by running noisily through the undergrowth. Polecats are common, but most likely to be seen as a roadside accident victim than as a live animal, while the sky is rarely empty of wheeling eagles and vultures searching for young rabbits and other prey.

History

6000BC
Earliest known villages on Crete; neolithic pottery and figurines.

around 3000BC
Migrants to Crete bring bronze-making technology and establish the first Minoan settlements. The beginning of the pre-Palatial period.

2200BC
First peak sanctuaries and use of hieroglyphic script.

2000BC
Beginning of the Old Palace period; palaces are built at Knosós, Faistós and Mália. First wheel-turned pottery and evidence of extensive trade links with Egypt and the Aegean islands.

1700BC
Earthquake destroys the old palaces. New palaces are built on top of the old. Beginning of the New Palace period to which most of the upstanding Minoan palaces, villas and villages on Crete belong. First fresco paintings.

1650BC
First use of Linear A script.

1550BC
The artistic peak of Minoan pottery and fresco.

1500BC
The eruption of the volcano on Théra (Santorini) to which the end of Minoan civilisation was attributed by 19th-century archaeologists.

1450BC
Fire on a massive scale brings a very sudden end to Minoan civilisation, destroying many palaces and villages. Beginning of the post-Palatial period during which Minoan culture was kept alive in isolated regions for another 400 years.

1400BC
Taking advantage of the disastrous situation on Crete, Mycenaeans (also known as Achaians) take over the island. The Minoan Linear A script is adapted to the Greek language to create Linear B. Weapons and warrior graves are found on Crete for the first time.

1050BC
Dorian Greeks arrive in Crete and establish many small and independent states, the origin of most of today's Cretan towns and villages.

650BC
Extensive trade with Egypt is reflected in the Egyptian influence on Dorian-period art.

450BC
The Law Code of Górtina is carved in stone.

69–67BC
Quintus Metellus invades Crete and ruthlessly destroys many towns and villages. The city of Górtina becomes the new capital of Roman Crete. The island is exploited for its grain but enjoys a period of peace and prosperity.

AD50
St Paul visits Crete and soon after sends St Titus to convert the island's inhabitants to Christianity.

395
With the Roman Empire split into eastern and western parts, Crete comes under eastern Byzantine control and the island's first churches are established.

824
Crete is invaded by the Arabs who use the island as a base for piratical attacks from their base in Al-Khandak, later to be called Iráklio.

961

Crete is liberated from the Arabs by the Byzantine general, Nikeforas Fokas. The beginning of Byzantine art and culture on the island.

1204

Venice diverts the Fourth Crusade to her own ends: the conquest of Byzantium. Crete is given to one of the Crusade leaders, Boniface of Montferrat, as his share in the spoils of the war, and he sells the island to Venice.

1263

The first of many revolts against Venetian rule; as a punishment, the villages of the Lasíthiou plateau are forcibly depopulated and nobody is allowed to farm the area for 200 years.

1453

Constantinople falls to the Turks and Byzantine scholars seek refuge in Crete, marking the beginning of the Cretan Renaissance in art, poetry and icon painting.

1645

The Turks begin their long assault on Crete, taking Khaniá and Réthimnon.

1669

Crete finally falls to the Turks. Under Turkish rule, rebellion becomes a way of life, leading to tribal opposition from remote mountain strongholds.

1821–32

The Greek War of Independence leads to the creation of the Greek state, but Crete is excluded.

1841

The first of a series of revolts in Crete in support of Enosis – union with Greece. Rebellion against the Turks, and harsh reprisals, continues for another 50 years.

1898

Britain, France, Russia and Italy occupy Crete and force the Ottoman Turks to recognise Crete's right to autonomy.

Prince George of Greece is installed as the island's governor.

1900

Arthur Evans begins excavating Knosós.

1913

The Turks are forced to surrender sovereignty over Crete and full union with Greece is achieved.

1941

Massive casualties are sustained on both sides during the infamous Battle of Crete. Cretans mount heroic resistance against the occupying German forces and suffer appalling reprisals as a result.

1945

The Liberation of Crete. Reconstruction of the Cretan economy gets under way. Tourism is negligible, with less than 400 foreign visitors a year.

1983

Mass tourism arrives on Crete, with visitor numbers exceeding 1 million (double the Cretan population) for the first time.

Manoliz Kazanis, clan leader during the 1821 War of Independence

The Minoans

Crete is the birthplace of Europe's oldest civilisation, though no-one suspected this until the late 19th century when foreigners were first given permission to conduct limited excavations on the island. Early archaeologists were astounded to discover, not the classical Greek sites they had been expecting, but the accomplished art and architecture of a far older civilisation, comparable in achievement with the other great ancient civilisations of China, Egypt and Mesopotamia.

Priests, kings and matriarchs

Arthur Evans (see page 58) called this culture Minoan after Minos, the legendary king of Crete. Scholars now believe that Minos was not the name of one man, but the title given to all rulers, like the Egyptian term, Pharaoh. Minoan rulers were also priests, and their palaces (at Knosós, Mália, Faistós and Zákros) were centres for elaborate rituals, in which acrobatic bull-leaping had an important part to play.

This was just one feature of their many-faceted religion: women clearly played an important role, and two of the commonest finds from Minoan temples and peak sanctuaries are clay figures of the bare-breasted Snake Goddess and figures of male devotees with erect penises or large codpieces. Olive trees, which frequently figure in Minoan frescos and on seals, were also worshipped. All this lends weight to the theory that Minoan religion was rooted in the cycle of the seasons, and that the palaces were centres of annual fertility rituals designed to ensure the success of the crops, probably involving bulls as sacrificial animals.

The west façade and grand staircase of the palace at Faistós

Old and New Palaces

In Minoan chronology, the Old Palace period, from 2000 to 1700BC, saw the development of massive palaces built around a courtyard, surrounded by clusters of smaller houses and workshops. In 1700BC an earthquake brought these elaborate palaces tumbling down. During the New Palace period, from 1700 to 1450BC, the palaces were rebuilt, on the same site, but more elaborate than before, with delicate frescos and fine furnishings.

The Bull's Head Rhyton in Iráklio's Archaeological Museum

Resources and revolution

Minoan society was highly organised, and the power of the priests was based on their control of precious commodities, such as olive oil. Oil was kept in vast quantities in huge jars (*pithoi*) in palace storerooms. Seal stones were used to mark the ownership of these jars, and clay tablets were used for making inventories and keeping accounts. The presence of such a large quantity of inflammable oil contributed greatly to the final destruction of the Minoan civilisation in 1450BC when fire swept through the palaces.

The evidence of the fires is plain for everyone to see when they visit Minoan palace sites, but the precise cause is shrouded in speculation and mystery. Evans confidently blamed the eruption of Théra, but that took place in 1500BC,

50 years previously. Other historians have put forward the theory that Crete was invaded and sacked, perhaps by the Mycenaeans who later came to control Crete, but there is no archaeological evidence to support this. One possible explanation is that the Minoans themselves toppled their rulers in a co-ordinated palace revolution.

Struggling on

In the post-palatial period, from 1450 to 1100BC, the Mycenaeans took advantage of the disaster that befell Crete and moved in, briefly occupying the palace at Knosós and using it as the administrative centre of the island until 1200BC when the palace was finally abandoned. Some peak sanctuaries continued in use, and there are echoes of the Minoan golden age in the Mycenaean-influenced sculpture and pottery of this era.

Some Cretans clung on to the old ways for generations; they are mentioned in Homer's *Odyssey* (written down around 700BC) where, in enumerating the various races who live on Crete, he mentions the 'Etocretans (ie the true, or genuine, Cretans), proud of their native stock'. Right up until the 3rd century BC they maintained their own separate language and script – leaving behind a number of mysterious and intriguing inscriptions, none of which have yet been deciphered, that have been found at Praisós and Dréros.

Politics

*C*retans are a fiercely proud and independent-minded people who, in the words of a popular phrase, see themselves as 'Cretans first, Greeks second'. They are also fond of naming their children Elifthérios (Freedom) and of quoting the patriotic slogan, 'Freedom or Death' that anti-Turkish rebels adopted as their battle cry in the 19th century (Kazantzákis later used it as the title for one of his novels). In reality, Cretans have experienced little in the way of true political freedom over the last 3,500 years.

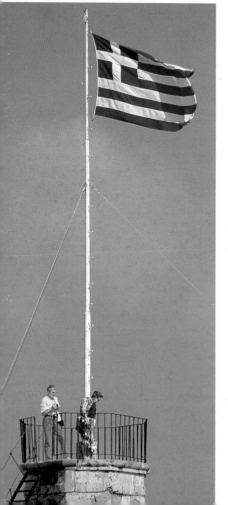

A history of oppression

Since the collapse of the Minoan civilisation in 1450BC, the island has been ruled by one foreign power after another – Mycenaeans, Dorian Greeks, Romans, Arabs, Byzantines, Venetians, Turks and Egyptians. The 20th century brought long-awaited unification with the rest of Greece, and the Cretan statesman, Elifthérios Venizélos, served as prime minister of Greece on numerous occasions, playing a central role in national politics and foreign affairs between 1896 and 1935. Soon after came civil war (between monarchists and republicans), followed by world war and invasion by Germany (see page 111). Post-war rule by military dictatorship kept Crete impoverished and isolated until the fall of the Greek colonels in 1974. Only then did Greece, along with Crete, become a parliamentary democracy, headed by a president (the monarchy was abolished following a popular referendum the same year).

National government

Even now, Crete has little political autonomy, for Greece has a strongly centralised government, with a parliament in Athens. Crete sends elected representatives, called deputies, to the

The flag of Greece

parliament, and one Cretan politician, Kostas Mitsotakis, rose to lead the right-of-centre ND (Néa Dhimokratía, or New Democracy) party, which narrowly won the 1990 election. Despite his Cretan birth, Mitsotakis commands less than full support from his fellow islanders, the majority of whom support the PASOK party (the Pan Hellenic Socialist Movement) whose sunrise symbol can be seen daubed on roads, embankments and bridges all over Crete. The corruption scandals that have muddied the party's reputation over recent years do not seem to have dimmed Cretan enthusiasm.

Local government

Crete has no independent regional government, and is ruled instead by governors appointed by the ruling party in Athens. There is one governor for each of the island's four provinces (*nomoi*), namely Khaniá, Réthimnon, Iráklio and Lasíthiou. In the past, Cretan governors and political leaders have modelled themselves on the clan leaders of old, whose proud portraits look down from the walls of the history museums in Khaniá and Iráklio. Refusing to be 'yes men' they have frequently defied the national party line in the greater interests of Crete. That is changing however and the availability of new development funds from the European Union means that their energies are focused on securing the maximum benefit for the island's road-building, health and educational projects.

Crete as a military base

Cretans love to disagree with each other on most subjects, and the presence of large numbers of NATO military personnel and weaponry in Soúdha Bay (Ormos Soúdhas) and on the Akrotíri

Above: Cretans love a debate
Below: the PASOK party's sunrise symbol

peninsula is one source of controversy. The NATO presence brings wealth to the island but Cretans are only too well aware that they stand between the Islamic world and the west, and are therefore a potential target in the event of aggression. Only one thing prevents Cretans from demanding an end to the NATO presence – the thought that Turkey (the old enemy) might offer NATO a new home, thus gaining valuable military and economic aid at Crete's expense.

Culture

On Crete two separate cultures co-exist side by side: the Crete of the 20th century and the rural, pre-industrial Crete, which has not changed much, in any essential respect, since Minoan times.

Country life

In the heart of rural Crete there are still many people, mainly elderly now, who live a very meagre, self-sufficient life. Their food comes from what they grow, or simply gather wild. Their simple homes have no electricity or television, and cooking is done over a wood fire. They rarely travel far beyond their home village, and when they do, they go by donkey, which also serves as an all-purpose pack animal.

These people are the survivors of the old Cretan way of life. Their children have left this (and them) behind, seeking paid work and an air-conditioned apartment in one of Crete's burgeoning towns, or emigrating to work on a building site or in a Greek restaurant far from home. The remaining rural Cretans claim to have an egalitarian society, without class distinctions or rancour, and the warm-heartedness of their easy-going hospitality appears to bear this out. They attribute their way of life to centuries of subjugation to foreign rulers, especially the harsh and oppressive Turks. Taxed into abject poverty and denied education or legal rights, they developed their own unwritten codes of honour, mutual respect and co-operation that have survived to this day.

The *kafenion*

Within this society, the *kafenion*, or café, also serves the purpose of local

Traditional farming

parliament. The typical village *kafeníon* is as plain as can be: no posters adorn the walls and there are no price lists or tempting bottles of exotic drinks on display. Local wine, coffee and water are the principal drinks on offer, and customers can linger for hours over one small drink and nobody will object. On the contrary, it would be thought odd not to linger, since the *kafeníon* is the local club, a place where men can gather to spend the whole evening in talk or play a game of backgammon. Cafés are traditionally male-dominated establishments.

Both club and parliament, the *kafeníon* is a male-dominated institution

The *voltá*

Women have their equivalent in the *voltá*, the evening stroll, a habit influenced by the Italian *passeggiata*, introduced by the Venetians. The *voltá* takes place at that delightful hour of the day when darkness begins to fall and work is done. As the sun sets and the swifts flit above the tree tops, soon to be replaced by the bats, housewives take off their aprons, brush their hair and step out of doors to see what is going on. Taking their children they stroll arm in arm to greet old friends, to gossip or, if they are still young and single, to flirt.

Country meets town

The *voltá* and the *kafeníon* are the two traditions that still link the old Crete with the new. The evening stroll in Réthimnon is especially vibrant, and the large number of students in both Khaniá and Réthimnon help to ensure that the cafés used by local people are always full – especially late at night, long after hard-working rural Cretans have gone to bed. Country rarely meets town except for village festivities, weddings, baptisms and funerals, or on the one day a week (often a Saturday) when rural Cretans descend on their nearest big town to set up street stalls selling everything from honey, olives and dried herbs to leather boots and hand-knitted sweaters. Arriving the night before market day, many give up the attempt to snatch some sleep in the back of their van or pick-up truck, drifting instead to the local cafés where the music and dancing go on until the first light of dawn.

Customs and etiquette

Cretan people are very friendly, if a little shy, on meeting stangers. A wave or a nod as you pass someone while out walking usually elicits a broad smile. If you say hello in Greek, all the better. Don't be surprised to be offered a piece of fruit off somebody's orange tree or a glass of *raki* on the house in a restaurant – or even a little extra dish you did not order. Such spontaneous generosity is still quite common, especially in the parts of Crete not tainted by mass tourism. Cretans love to practise their English, so take the time to chat – about the weather, children, your job – all are subjects of endless potential.

Cretan Costume

*C*retan costume is still worn with pride by some country Cretans, especially by the older men who gather to pass the day playing backgammon in the *kafeníon*. Prior to the Turkish occupation of Crete, dress consisted of a simple belted tunic for both men and women. Examples can be seen in many church frescos throughout the island. Typically, the donor of the fresco (and his wife) is depicted beside the door of the church, and these portraits show that costume changed little in the period from the 11th to the 16th century (copies of these are displayed in Iráklio's Historical Museum – see page 36).

Turkish fashions

The Turks introduced baggy breeches (called *raki*) which Cretans adopted in a major break with their past. Ironically it was the anti-Turkish rebels who were keenest on this new fashion (today, Cretan men are more likely to wear ordinary riding breeches). Waistcoats are worn over a simple shirt by men and women alike, usually embroidered with colourful motifs that differ from region to region. Women also wear skirts of brightly coloured stripes, protected by a simple apron. Men adopted the black crochet-work cap with its distinctive fringe as a symbol of mourning for their island under Turkish occupation, though the cap continues to be worn to this day.

Dressed in their best for a wedding or festival

Daggers and boots

On special occasions (such as weddings and feast days), men still wear a big silk sash around their waist, into which they tuck a whole collection of heirlooms – perhaps a tobacco horn, prerhaps a silver dagger or a pistol (often an antique weaponof 18th-century date last used in World War II). Smart and highly polished riding boots complete the picture, along with a moustache. Fine examples of historic costume are displayed in the Historical Museums at Iráklio (see page 36), Khaniá (see page 95) and at the Museum of Cretan Ethnology in Vorí (see page 76).

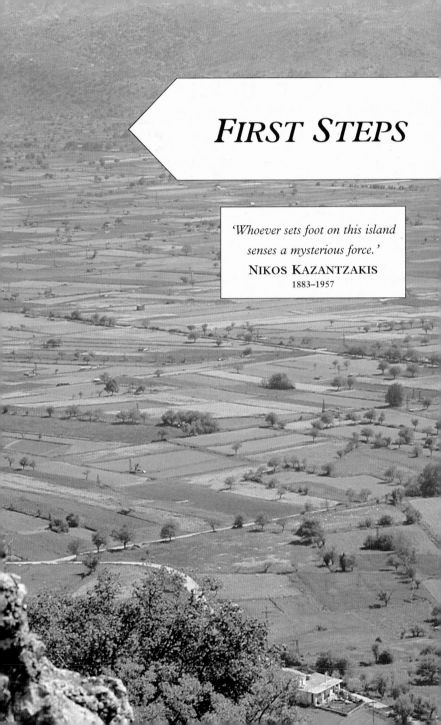

FIRST STEPS

'*Whoever sets foot on this island senses a mysterious force.*'
NIKOS KAZANTZAKIS
1883–1957

First Steps

*T*he idea of touring Crete by car and stopping somewhere different every night has yet to catch on. The lack of direct scheduled flights to Crete means that you are virtually forced to travel on a package, booking your accommodation in advance. A few specialist tour operators offer fly-drive holidays, but even they insist that you spend a minimum of three nights in each of the hotels of your choice.

Island wandering is really only feasible during the quieter times of the year, when flight-only deals are available and when hotels have rooms to spare. Fortunately this coincides with the spring and autumn, when flowers are most abundant and when the temperatures are ideal for walking.

East or west, north or south?

An alternative to going wherever you please is to choose one hotel or villa that is centrally located for the area you want to explore. This means basing yourself in the north of the island where the national highway provides a relatively swift route from east to west. Even so, Crete is far too large to see in one week, or even in a fortnight. The best you can hope to do in two weeks is to explore the eastern or the western half of the island, choosing your base accordingly.

The east of Crete is best for those who want to see the main archaeological sites. To explore this region, you could do worse than choose a base on the coastal strip between Iráklio and Áyios Nikólaos. Here you will be within easy reach of the palaces at Knosós, Mália, Faistós and Zákros, and within easy driving distance of the Lasíthiou plateau and Dhíktaen Cave (Dhiktaio Andro). Be warned, though, that this is the most developed part of Crete, so you have to choose your base carefully, paying more, perhaps, for a villa in a village rather than ending up in a cheap but anonymous apartment in one of the tourist ghettos, such as Mália and Khersónisos.

Hiking and flowers

The further west you go on Crete, the quieter it gets, although there is another flurry of tourist development around Khaniá. Western Crete is generally greener, more mountainous and less intensively farmed than the plains that make up so much of eastern Crete. Nature lovers will find that the west is far richer, botanically, and for historically

Scooters, and cars, can be hired in nearly every town or resort

Cruising to Eloúndha

inclined visitors, there is a greater concentration of Byzantine churches to explore. Above all, this is the region for long and spectacular walks through the Samaria and Ímbros gorges (Farangi Samariás and Farangi Ímvrokiko), or out along the finger-like peninsulas of the northern coast.

Beach holidays

If you just want to drop out and do nothing more energetic than strolling to the beach each day, there are scores of semi-tropical hideaways in the less-developed extremities of the island, from Vái, in the extreme east of the island, to the Elafonísi islands in the extreme west. Most are on the south side of the island, with characterful fishing villages such as Palaiókhora, Khóra Sfakíon and Mátala scoring highly because of their unspoilt Cretan character combined with good restaurants, shops and nightlife. The amount of accommodation available in these villages is very limited, so you will have to book early in the season, using the tour operators who specialise in the less well-known parts of the island.

Getting around

If you know you want to do a lot of touring on Crete, it is cheaper to pre-book a hire car as part of your holiday package. However, if you decide to wait until you arrive in Crete, you will find scores of car rental agents on the main street of every Cretan town.

It is vital to check the state of the tyres (including the spare) before setting out on any journey, and be sure that you know how to use the jack – potholes and sharp stones make it easy to suffer a puncture on Crete's rural roads. Motorbikes and scooters are also readily available for hire, but are not suitable for long journeys. Despite the fact that many Cretans break the law, wearing a helmet is compulsory – ensure that the hire company gives you one that fits you comfortably and is not damaged.

Museums and archaeological sites

Cretans are early risers, making the most of the coolest part of the day and taking a long siesta during the afternoon. Opening times reflect this, with many museums and sites open for the morning and early afternoon only (typically 8.30am–3pm). Photography is allowed in museums and on sites, but you usually have to pay a small fee in addition to the entrance charge, with higher fees for video cameras and tripods. At Knosós (where the site guards are unusually truculent, and prone to go on strike very regularly to protest about their grievances) you may not even be allowed to carry a camera on to the site without paying the extra fee. Officially it is forbidden to climb on the walls at archaeological sites, but this rule is widely ignored. You will also find that sites are, quite literally, littered with ancient pottery sherds – picking them up is also against the law, as is any kind of unlicensed digging.

Rural churches are often open all the time

Monasteries and churches

Monasteries are generally open to visitors from 8am to 1pm or 2pm, though some reopen at 3pm or 5pm until 7pm. All insist on modest dress (shorts, sleeveless shirts and beachwear are forbidden) so it is sensible to carry a change of clothes if you go visiting a monastery.

The opening arrangements for churches vary considerably. Some are open all the time, but many are kept locked. It is common practice to begin the hunt for the key (*to kleidí*) at the nearest *kafenion* (café), but it is not good manners to do so during the 1pm–5pm siesta hours. Often the key is held by the local priest (*pappás*) who may accompany you to the church and provide an enthusiastic guided commentary, in broken English, on the principal frescos and icons. If so, you will be expected to give the priest a small donation towards church funds. Remember, too, that women are not supposed to enter the sanctuary (the area behind the iconostasis, or screen) unless invited.

WHAT TO SEE

'A little bird sings
On top of Psíloriti:
"Another island isn't found
In all the world like Kriti" '
CRETAN SONG

Eastern Crete

*E*astern Crete is made up of the two provinces (*nomoi*) of Iráklio and Lasíthiou. This is the most heavily populated part of the island, with 263,868 people living in Iráklio province (127,600 of them in Iráklio city alone) and 70,762 in Lasíthiou (8,000 in the capital, Áyios Nikólaos). Together these two provinces account for over 60 per cent of the total Cretan population of 536,180.

The resort coast

The city of Iráklio is the main gateway to the island, with a ferry port and international airport. Around 70 per cent of the 1.8 million tourists who come to Crete every year stay in one of the resorts strung out along the 70km coastal strip that lies between the two provincial

EASTERN CRETE

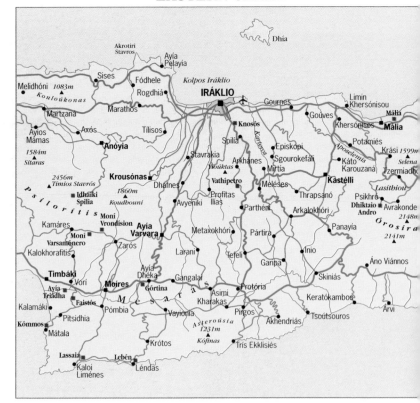

Lake Voulisméni, in Áyios Nikólaos

capitals, especially the resort towns of
Khersónisos, Mália, Eloúndha and Áyios
Nikólaos. Staying in any of these places
you will not lack for shops, cocktail bars,
nightlife or the company of fellow
visitors, but you will experience very little
of the true Crete.

Beaches

The coastal strip east of Iráklio is one
long series of resorts, many of them

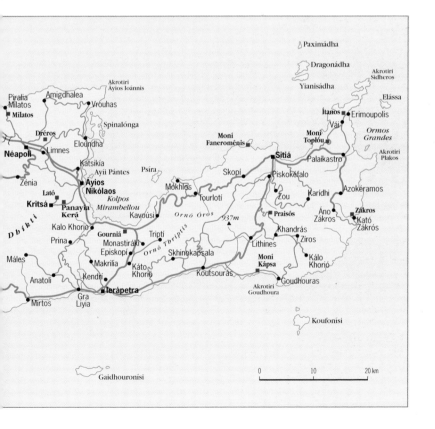

Yachts and fishing boats moor beneath the protecting walls of Iráklio's Venetian Fort

offering shops, fast-food outlets and beach loungers for hire. If you want to escape the crowds, head for the far east of the island, or the less developed beaches on the south coast. Remoteness does not guarantee isolation, however: the so-called Palm Beach at Vaí, and the nudist beach at Préveli, are among the most crowded on the island at the peak of the season.

Reputations undeserved
Both provincial capitals have suffered at the hands of writers who have exaggerated their less attractive features. Iráklio is often portrayed as the ultimate urban jungle of dusty and noisy streets and bumper-to-bumper horn-blowing traffic. For much of the time Iráklio is, in fact, a quiet and surprisingly civilised city with a characterful open-air market, much interesting (if dilapidated) architecture and an archaeological museum whose contents can compete with the best that Greece has to offer.

Áyios Nikólaos has also been ill-served by press and politicians who have dubbed it the 'lager-lout capital of Europe', but this is by no means a town of rabid hooligans on the rampage – rather it is Eastern Crete's most picturesque town, set around a natural lake, with many excellent restaurants and shops.

The Mesarás Plain

It was here, on the flat and fertile agricultural plain of Mesarás, that the Minoan civilisation first arose and where the most spectacular archaeological sites are to be found. Three of the four major Minoan palaces, which formed the focal point for Minoan art and industry, are located here (at Knosós, Mália and Faistós), along with smaller palace complexes at Ayía Triádha, Gourniá and Arkhánes.

Lasíthiou

The other important Minoan palace is at Zákros, in Lasíthiou province, at the extreme eastern end of the island. Lasíthiou is a mountainous province, famous as the birthplace of the mighty Zeus. His mother, Rhea, sought out the privacy of the Dhíktaen Cave for her confinement so that the infant god might not suffer the same fate as his siblings and be eaten by their father, Kronos (see page 34). Today there is little privacy to be had at the cave, which has become one of the major tourist attractions on Crete, featuring on coach excursions along with the windmill-covered Lasíthiou plain, which sits in a bowl, entirely encircled by high peaks, just to the south of Mália.

The south coast

This being Crete, the opportunity to escape from the crowds is never very far away, and true solitude can be experienced on the southern coast, much of which is accessible only by dirt roads and footpaths. Here, adventurous travellers can track down hermits' caves and monasteries clinging to the cliffs.

How long this will continue to be true remains to be seen. Bulldozers have already begun to open up a new south coast road and concrete villas are spreading rapidly around any tiny village with access to a sandy beach. Against this tide of development attempts are being made to establish a national park around Koutsourás. Sadly, arsonists have burned down much of the natural pine forest that was to form the focal point of the park, and new saplings are regularly cut down or uprooted by local villagers who want to build holiday villas and polythene tunnels for fruit and vegetables listed.

Streets and workshops in the ancient Minoan town of Gourniá

Iráklio

*I*ráklio is the fifth largest city in Greece, with a population of 115,000. The air raids of 1941 reduced the city to rubble so that it lacks the old-world charm of Réthimnon or Khaniá. Though no great beauty, Iráklio can at least claim to be prosperous, with the highest per capita income of any city in Greece, derived from a combination of shipping, banking and tourism. The city's star attraction is the Archaeological Museum (see page 30) full of Minoan treasures, many excavated at Knosós (see page 52) just 5km to the south.

Iráklio's historic fort and harbour

THE HARBOUR

Iráklio's historic harbour bustles with luxury yachts and fishing boats unloading their catch beneath the

IRÁKLIO TOWN PLAN

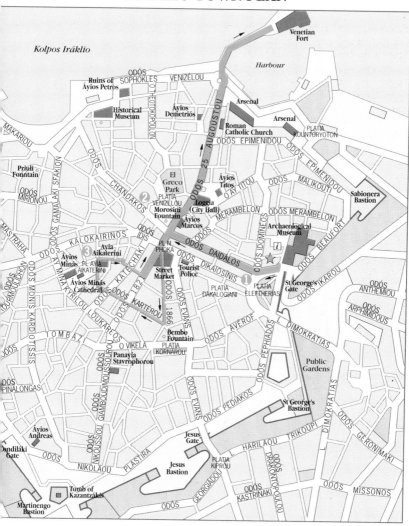

Kolpos Iráklio

Venetian Fort

Harbour

ODÓS SOPHOKLES VENIZÉLOU

Ruins of Áyios Petros

Historical Museum

Áyios Demetriós

Arsenal

Arsenal

Roman Catholic Church

PLATÍA KOUNTORYOTON

ODÓS EPIMENIDOU

MAKARIOU

ODÓS 25 AUGOUSTOU

Priuli Fountain

ODÓS MIRIONOU

ODÓS GAMALAKI SFAKION

CHANDAKOS

El Greco Park

PLATÍA VENIZÉLOU Morosini Fountain

Áyios Títos

O AY TITOU

ODÓS MALIKOUTI

ODÓS EPIMENIDOU

Sabionera Bastion

MASTRAHA

ODÓS KALOKAIRINOS

ODÓS IDIS

Loggia (City Hall)

Áyios Márcos

MERAMBELON

ODÓS MERAMBELON

ODÓS IDOMINEOS

Archaeological Museum

ODÓS BEAUFORT

Áyios Minás

Ayía Aikateríni

PL AYIA AIKATERINI

KATECHAK

PL N PHOKÁ

ODÓS DAIDÁLOS

ODÓS DIKAIOSÍNIS

i

St George's Gate

ODÓS IKAROU

ODÓS ANTHEMIOU

Áyios Minás Cathedral

ODÓS MONIS KARDIOTISSIS

AX MAKARTRILOU

ODÓS 1821

Street Market

Tourist Police

PLATÍA DAKALOGIANI

PLATÍA ELEFTHERIAS

ODÓS ARPHIMIDOUS

ODÓS KARTEROU

ODÓS 1866

ODÓS EVANS

DIMOKRATIAS

TOMBAZ

O VIKELA

LOUKAREOS

Bembo Fountain

PLATÍA KORNAROU

ODÓS AVEROF

ODÓS PEPHIADOS

Public Gardens

ODÓS PINALONGAS

ODÓS GIAMBOUDMOUSSOUROU

Panayía Stavrophorou

ODÓS EVANS

ODÓS PEDIAKOS

St George's Bastion

DIMOKRATIAS

ODÓS GERONIMAKI

Áyios Andreas

ODÓS NIKOUSSIOU

Jesus Gate

HARILAOU

TRIKOUPI

andiláki Gate

ODÓS NIKOLAOU

PLASTIRA

Jesus Bastion

PLATÍA KIPROU

ODÓS GEORGIADOU

ODÓS DRAKONTOPOULOU

ODÓS KASTRINAKI

ODÓS MISSONOS

Tomb of Kazantzákis

Martinengo Bastion

protecting walls of the bulky Venetian fort. The first fort was built here in 1303 but this was later destroyed by an earthquake. The fort was rebuilt in between 1523 and 1540, and was to play a key role in the Great Siege of 1647–69. At the end of this 21-year siege, one of the longest in history, the Venetians finally gave up one of their most precious possessions, surrendering Iráklio (and Crete) to the Turks, but only after heroic resistance, in which 30,000 Venetians and 118,000 Turks met their deaths. The new Turkish rulers of Iráklio changed little, and even the Lion of St Mark, symbol of Venice, still stands guard over the entrance to the fort.

Another legacy of Venetian rule is the 16th-century Arsenal where ships of the Venetian naval fleet were once built, repaired and fitted out for battle. A busy new road has since cut these huge vaulted buildings off from the harbour, but they remain an impressive tribute to Venetian marine engineering.
Venetian fort: open April to October, Tuesday to Sunday 8.30am–3pm. Admission charge.

THE RAMPARTS AND TOMB OF KAZANTZÁKIS

Contemporary with the Fort and the Arsenal are the walls that enclose Iráklio for a total length of 3km. It is possible to walk the complete circuit for views of city

IRÁKLIO'S NAME

The bustling capital of Crete started out as a Minoan harbour, named Heraclium by the Romans. In 824, under Saracen rule, it became Rabdh el Khanadak (Castle of the Ditch), was corrupted to Khandakas and later, under Venetian rule, to Candia. This was the name under which the city, and the whole island, was known until the end of Turkish rule in 1898 when the Roman name was revived, but in the Greek version, to give the name Heraklion (Iráklio in modern Greek spelling).

gardens and rooftops, but in order to gain a sense of the massive proportions of the walls it is best to visit Porta Kenoúria, the gate on Odós Evans in the south of the city. Built in 1538 by the great Italian architect, Michele Sanmicheli, the walls stand 18m tall and over 40m thick. On the Martinengo Bastion, five minutes walk to the southwest, is the simple grave of the Cretan novelist, Níkos Kazantzákis (see page 67). He was buried here at his own request and the inscription on his tomb says much about the Cretan attitude to life and mortality: 'I hope for nothing, I fear nothing, I am free.'

ARCHAEOLOGICAL MUSEUM

This is rated one of the top museums in Greece because of the quality of the objects on display. The sheer number of visitors can be a problem so allow longer than you would expect to tour the museum, or come during the lunch hour when there are many fewer tour groups.

Room I

This room is devoted to the neolithic and pre-palatial phase of Cretan history (6000–2000BC). Here we see the first depictions of bulls and acrobats, of the female fertility deity with exaggerated hips, breasts and buttocks, of the symbolic double-bladed axe, and of the moclos – the sacred double horn emblem. These motifs recur again and again, honed and refined over 3,000 years of production.

Among the assorted exhibits, the highlights are the pottery rattle (between Cases 4 and 5), with a tracing alongside of the scene from the Harvester Cup (see Room VII), showing such a rattle in use; and the wonderfully naturalistic pot lid in Case 7 with a handle shaped like a dog.

Rooms II and III

These two rooms are devoted to the Old Palace period (2000–1700BC). A delightful insight into the sophistication of architecture at the time is given by the so-called Town Mosaic (Case 25), consisting of a number of pottery squares painted with representations of Minoan houses. There are numerous clay figurines from peak sanctuaries, pointing to their heads or stomachs, perhaps indicating bits of their bodies that they want curing. Woman wear bell-shaped skirts and place their hands under their breasts, pushing them up in a gesture of offering, whilst men have erect penises or large codpieces.

Room III contains masterpieces of Minoan pottery, such as the vase with the daisy motif (Case 36) and the lifelike clay pig in the last case on the right. Here too is the famous circular clay disk from Faistós, bearing a stamped inscription that has so far defeated all attempts at interpretation.

Room IV

This is the first of six rooms devoted to the New Palace period (1700–1450BC), with outstanding works from

The famous Faistós disc remains an enigma

the palace at Knosós. One is a gaming board made of ivory and precious stone (Case 57). In Case 49 is a lovely vase covered in an all-over pattern of bamboo leaves. Case 51 contains the famous Bull's Head Rhyton, a gentle looking beast carved out of steatite, with gilded wooden horns, rock crystal eyes and inlaid shell nostrils. Sacred libations – perhaps of bull's blood or wine – were poured from holes around his mouth.

Case 56 contains a delicate ivory figure of an acrobat flying through the air in mid-manoeuvre, probably having launched himself from the horns of a bull. Case 52 is full of stone vases covered in intricate designs – see the one entitled 'The Entrapped Octopus', for example.

Case 50 brings us face to face with the Snake Goddess, a frightening figure when viewed close up, with bulging eyes that seek to entrance the onlooker – or is it the goddess herself that is in a trance? Next to her is another similar figure crawling with snakes that entwine her hair, dress and belt.

The entrancing figure of the Snake Goddess

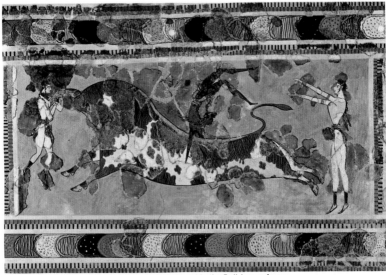

The agility and self-confidence of youth is captured in the Bull-leaper fresco

Room V

This room contains material excavated from parts of Knosós away from the main palace, including the workshops and houses lining the Royal Road. An idea of what these houses may have looked like is indicated by the clay model in Case 70A. Pictures on the walls of this room show reconstructions of various parts of Knosós drawn by Piet de Jong, the draughtsman who worked with Sir Arthur Evans during the excavation of the site.

Room VI

Here the most rewarding exhibits are in the central cases, where gold and ivory jewellery is displayed, including necklace ornaments and rings shaped like shells, bulls' heads, lions and ducks.

Room VII

This contains the finest example of Minoan jewellery ever found, an exquisite pendant of gold depicting two bees, joined at the mouth and tail, holding a honeycomb between their legs (Case 101). Equally enthralling are three stone vases. The subject of the Chieftain Cup (Case 95) is still being debated: does it show a hunting party, or a Minoan chieftain being presented with hides as some form of tax or tribute? The Boxer Rhyton (Case 96) shows the now-familiar sport of bull-leaping, as well as scenes of boxing and wrestling. The marvellous Harvester Vase (Case 94) shows a procession of youths carrying rods and pitchforks, accompanied by singers and musicians, one brandishing a rattle, taking part in some kind of harvest festival.

Room VIII

The finest of all the Minoan libation vases is the Peak Sanctuary Rhyton (Case 111). Not only is the carving wonderfully naturalistic, with wild tulips blossoming from the craggy heights, Cretan goats with magnificent horns resting on the mountain ridges, and crows using the sacred bull's horn symbol on the temple roof as a perch, it also provides a detailed view of the appearance of a Minoan peak sanctuary of the type otherwise known only from excavated ruins.

Also in this room are numerous fine examples of pottery shaped like shells or decorated with marine motifs, such as waves, seaweed or starfish.

Room IX

The marine motifs continue with an especially enjoyable octopus flask to be found in Case 120.

Rooms X to XIII

Exhibits dating to the post-Minoan era (1100–500BC) show new developments and the introduction of Egyptian influences to Minoan art. Though the objects are more primitive and the decoration more debased, there are some unusual figures, including the Poppy Goddess (Room X, Case 133) and the woman on a swing (Room X, Case 143). The displays on the ground floor end with a roomful of clay sarcophagi, shaped like bathtubs.

Rooms XIV to XVI

Much of the first floor of the museum is devoted to Minoan frescos, forming the highlight of the collection. The archaeologists who reconstructed these works, often from a tiny handful of fragments, have been accused of using their imaginations too freely, but it is difficult not to be moved by the great vibrancy and naturalism displayed by the Partridge Frieze, or the Leaping Dolphins. Problems of interpretation are well illustrated by the display in Room

XVI where a fresco, previously thought to depict a boy picking flowers (entitled the 'Saffron Gatherer') has now been reassembled to create a bigger picture called the 'Blue Monkey', set in a landscape of rocks and crocuses.

Completely original is the wonderful stone sarcophagus in the centre of Room XIV, its painted decoration of aquamarine blue and ox-blood red still remarkably fresh. The long sides depict a funeral procession in great detail, showing a horse-drawn chariot, the sacrifice of a young bull and various musical instruments.

Rooms XVII to XX

The last part of the museum is devoted to Greek and Roman antiquities, which seem almost lifeless compared with the exuberance of the preceding frescos. Only an occasional exhibit stands out, such as the life-size statue of a boy in bronze (Room XVIII), found at Ierápetra and dating from the 1st century BC.

Platía Eleftherías (tel: 081–226092). Open: Tuesday to Sunday 8am–7pm in summer, 8am–3pm in winter. Closed: Monday. Admission charge.

Clay model of a Minoan house

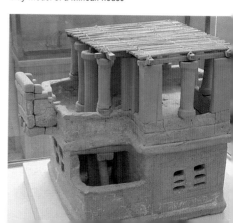

CRETAN MYTHS

The birth of Zeus

The myth begins in the time of the Titans, the primeval sons of Gaia (the Earth) and Uranus (the Heavens). Kronos (Time), the youngest of the Titans, had already dethroned his own father and castrated him in order to become king. Now, he was in the habit of swallowing his own children at birth to prevent them from robbing him of his kingship in turn.

Mightily fed up with the loss of five children, Rhea, the wife (and sister) of Kronos hid deep in the Dhíktaen cave on Crete to give birth to Zeus. Kronos got to hear of the birth and demanded his usual meal, but was given a stone wrapped in swaddling clothes instead. Zeus, meanwhile, was secreted in the Idhaean Cave where he was protected by his grandmother, Gaia.

Minos and the Minotaur

In time, Zeus came to overthrow his father and establish his throne on Mount Olympus. One day he fell in love with Europa, the granddaughter of Poseidon. He appeared in the guise of a bull, carried Europa away on his back and impregnated her. Europa gave birth to King Minos, who, with the guidance of his father, Zeus, ruled Crete wisely. His happiness was, however, shattered by Pasiphae, his licentious wife. She too fell in love with a white bull (this time not a god in disguise), and turned to Daidalos, artist and inventor, who built a wooden cow, covered in hide. In this disguise, Pasiphae was mounted by the bull. The fruit of this bestial union was the monstrous Minotaur, half-man, half-bull, who terrorised the court of King Minos until Daidalos invented an endless labyrinth, within which the beast was ensnared.

Theseus outwits the Minotaur

The Minotaur was given an annual diet of seven male and seven female virgins. One year, Prince Theseus, son of the Athenean king, Aegeus, intending to slay the Minotaur, volunteered to be one of the victims. On Crete, he was

taking Ariadne with him, though he subsequently abandoned her on the island of Naxos

When Theseus arrived back in Athens he forgot to hoist a white sail to signal his safe return. His father, Aegeus, assumed that his son had been killed by the Minotaur and leapt into the sea,which has been named the Aegean ever since in his honour.

Left: the infant Zeus
Above: Theseus slays the Minotaur
Right: Theseus and Ariadne

assisted by Ariadne, the daughter of King Minos, who gave him a sword and a ball of wool. Attaching one end of the wool to the door of the labyrinth, Theseus was able to retrace his steps and escape once he had killed the Minotaur. Theseus then set sail for Athens,

THE HISTORICAL MUSEUM OF CRETE

The Historical Museum is worth a visit if for no other reason than to see the only painting by El Greco to remain on the island of his birth. This is displayed on the ground floor, but first the museum attendants will usher you downstairs to begin a chronological tour of the museum in the basement.

Basement

Here are displayed sculptures and architectural fragments dating back to the Venetian occupation of the island. There are doorways and windows, angels, saints and coats of arms and tombstones that indicate the cosmopolitan nature of the island's port, bearing Turkish, Armenian and Jewish inscriptions.

Reconstruction of a typical Cretan home, with handmade furniture and a loom

Ground floor

Outstanding examples of Byzantine art are displayed on the ground floor, including a 13th-century apse fresco, one of the earliest to survive on the island, depicting the Virgin, St John and the Church Fathers, Nicholas and Basil. One area is devoted to a special exhibition on donors' portraits in medieval church frescos, and what these tell us about dress and fashions during the Byzantine era. Another room contains liturgical objects from ancient churches now either destroyed or converted to other uses, of which the most outstanding are the 6th-century candlesticks, crucifixes, pattens and chalices from the Early Christian church of Áyios Títos, at Górtina.

El Greco

El Greco's painting of the *Monastery of Saint Catherine on Mount Sinai* is given place of honour in its own darkened and air-conditioned room. This is no great masterpiece, but it is instantly recognisable as belonging to a different world from the precise Byzantine icons and stylised frescos that hang in the other rooms of the museum. There is an impressionistic quality about the brushwork: note the marvellous economy with which El Greco delineates the travelling Bedouin and his camel. The swirling yellow-pink clouds suggest some divine presence in the heavens and Mount Sinai seems to bend before an invisible wind. Altogether, the painting is suffused with a strange and unearthly light, suggestive of passion and emotion. The work betrays the influence of El Greco's teacher, Titian, who was himself one of the great Venetian masters who developed the use of light to heighten the drama of his paintings. El Greco – born in Iráklio in 1541 and christened Doménico Theotokópoulos – painted this work around 1570, and it marks a major stage in his transition from the Byzantine to the European style of art.

First floor

Harrowing documentary photographs bring home the human heroism and

El Greco's *Monastery of Saint Catherine on Mount Sinai*, his only surviving work on Crete

tragedy of World War II and the Battle of Crete (see page 110). The most vivid shows Emmanuel Katsenavas and his son facing execution for their resistance work – brave men visibly flinching in anticipation of the bullets that will shortly end their lives. Two contrasting studies are also reconstructed here – one belonging to Emmanuel Tsouderós, the Réthimnon-born prime minister of Greece at the time of the Battle of Crete, and the other to Níkos Kazantzákis, along with a display of his novels in various editions and languages.

Top floor
For many visitors, this will prove the most rewarding part of the museum, with cases devoted to Cretan folk art full of richly coloured rugs and beautifully embroidered bodices and waistcoats. One room is furnished as a typical Cretan home, with a beaten-earth floor, stone benches and clay oil lamps. You can admire examples of Cretan bagpipes and lyres, and a splendid example of wedding bread, elaborately decorated with fishes and fruits.

Odós Kalokerinov 7, opposite the Zenia Hotel, west of the Venetian Harbour. Tel: 081–283219. Open: Monday to Friday 9.30am–4.30pm, Saturday 9.30am–2.30pm. Closed: Sunday. Admission charge.

ICON COLLECTION, AYÍA AIKATERÍNI

Crete holds a very special place in the history of icon painting. It was to this island that many of the best practitioners of the art fled after Constantinople (modern Istanbul) fell to the Turks in 1453. The Byzantine Empire had been deeply conservative in all things, including painting. Artists jealously preserved antique painting styles and techniques, which they brought to Crete and passed on to pupils who were organised into schools and workshops, often attached to major monasteries.

Today's icon painters are keeping alive a centuries-old artistic tradition

East meets West

The church and monastery of Ayía Aikateríni, now the Icon Museum, was one of these schools. It was founded in 1555 when Crete was under Venetian rule and at almost precisely the same time as Venetian artists, such as Titian, Veronese and Tintoretto, were developing the High Renaissance style. Many Cretan artists studied for periods in Venetian workshops, and it was inevitable that there should be some cross-fertilisation between backward-looking Cretan icon painting and the Venetian avant garde. El Greco (see page 36) was one product of the meeting of the two cultures, and another was his near contemporary, Mikhaíl Damaskinós, whose works form the highlight of this small museum. Little is known about the life of Damaskinós, except that he studied in Venice in 1577–82, and that the icons displayed here were painted after his return to Crete, probably in the 1590s, for the monastery at Vrondísi (see page 80).

Italian style

The *Adoration of the Magi*, by Damaskinós, is an icon clearly influenced by Gozzoli's frescos in the Medici Chapel in Florence. The lavish use of gold and the stylisation of the mountains and drapery mark this as a Byzantine work, but the figures, their gestures,

ICONS AND MIRACLES

Icons are no mere pictures – to the faithful, they have miraculous powers, being a medium through which devotees can communicate with the saint or holy personage depicted – hence the votive offerings placed on or near icons by people seeking a cure for their complaints. Copies of miraculous icons have the same powers as the original – hence the practice of mass-producing icons and the inate conservatism of the art – worshippers want a precise copy, not artistic innovation. Perhaps that is why Damaskinós reverted to type in his later work – discarding all that he had learned from Renaissance artists.

expressions and postures are far more realistic than is normal in the iconic style. From Botticelli's painting of the *Nativity*, Damaskinós has taken the idea of including himself in the picture; he is the crowned king in scarlet cloak, staring directly and questioningly out of the picture at the onlooker – in this case a somewhat idealised and youthful portrait. The icon depicting *The Last Supper* shows the degree to which Damaskinós embraced the rules of perspective, using the architectural framework and the

As precious as a jewel, and widely held to have miraculous powers

table on which the supper is served to give his painting depth. His Apostles are all individual people, with thoughts, ideas and expressions of their own.

Back to Byzantine

By comparison, the four remaining icons by Damskinós show a reversion to the austerity and stylisation that is more typical of Byzantine icons. Faces are standardised and serenely emotionless. Several scenes are depicted at once, instead of the painting focusing on a single key event. In the *Virgin of the Burning Bush*, the central image is a symbolic one: the Virgin is burned but

not consumed – like gold in alchemy, she passes the test of absolute purity. *Noli me Tangere* shows the newly risen Christ appearing to the Holy Women while *The Nicaean Ecumenical Council* shows the church fathers meeting to settle fundamental issues of Christian belief. The *Divine Liturgy* shows Christ as the first priest celebrating Communion with a congregation of angels.

Platía Aikateríni. Currently closed for restoration work but normally open: Monday to Saturday, 9.30am–1pm; Tuesday, Thursday and Saturday, 5–7pm. Closed: Sunday. Admission charge.

The baroque belltower of Panayía Vatiótissa church in Arkhánes

from the 16th and 17th centuries. One shows the popular Cretan theme of the *Virgin as the Fount of Life* – the Virgin and Child stand in a fountain from which miracle-working waters flow.

Minoan Arkhánes

The scant remains of Minoan Arkhánes are not signposted, but are easy to reach. Walk up the square, towards the fork where the one-way system begins. Take the left fork, then first left. Turn left at the end of the street, then right. The next track on the right will take you to the locked gates of the site where you can glimpse the massive blocks of well-shaped masonry forming the theatral area, archive and reservoir of a major Minoan palace. The stone has turned pink from the fierce heat of the fire that destroyed the palace in 1450BC. Return to the main square, past houses built out of recycled Minoan masonry!

Fourní

Archaeologists cannot explore the palace site further because it lies beneath the modern town. They have, however, uncovered the huge cemetery at Fourní, on the town's outskirts. Reaching the site involves a long hard climb up a hill carpeted in wildflowers in spring.

Go back to the church and drive a short way out of the town, turn left by the large school and follow the signposted track until it ends; then follow the very steep track uphill to reach the site fence, following it to the left until you come to the entrance (normally open 8am–3pm). Whether you think the effort of getting there worthwhile depends on your attitude to views. Set on a rocky

ARKHÁNES

A good half day can be spent exploring the Minoan sites in and around Arkhánes, a prosperous agricultural town in the plain south of Iráklio, renowned for the quality of its grapes. These are blessed in a festival that takes place every 6 August, following a custom that dates back perhaps to Minoan times, whereby the first fruits of the harvest are offered to the gods.

Arkhánes is, in fact, two villages rather than one. Shortly after entering the first part, Páno Arkhánes, park in the main square with its walnut trees, shops, church and war memorial.

Panayía Vatiótissa church

The little triple-naved church with its baroque belltower contains a surprisingly rich collection of icons, many dating plateau high above the town, the views stretch endlessly across the fertile plain that underpinned Minoan prosperity. The most impressive tomb on this site lies some distance to the left of the entrance. Tholos Tomb A has a ceremonial approach ramp leading to the narrow entrance of a huge beehive-shaped chamber which must once have been visible from all over the valley. Archaeologists found the undisturbed remains of a princess here, still wearing her jewellery.

Arkhánes Archaeological Museum

To learn more about the cemetery, it is worth visiting this excellent new museum. Go back to the town, follow the one-way system until you reach a large café-lined square where you can park and walk, following signs to the museum. One of the principle exhibits here is a vivid reconstruction of the so-called human-sacrifice shrine at Anemóspili, 3km northwest of Arkhánes. Here archaeologists found controversial evidence that the Minoans practiced human sacrifice. In this case a young

man had been put to the knife in a last desperate attempt to avert the disastrous earthquake of 1700BC which, minutes later, destroyed not just the shrine, but all the palaces on Crete, marking the end of the Old Palace period.
Open: Wednesday to Monday 9am–2.30pm. Closed: Tuesday.

Vathípetro

Today the Anemóspili shrine is no more than a platform of stone (surrounded by a stinking landfill site) and not really worth a visit. Far more rewarding is the Minoan villa at Vathípetro, 5km south of Arkhánes This idyllic site is surrounded by vineyards, just as it was in the period 1700–1450BC when the villa was in use. The state of preservation is outstanding – you can even visit the original wine-making room with its clay presses and pans set out as if ready for the grape harvest to begin.
Open: 9am–2.30pm, except Monday.

Arkhánes is 16km south of Iráklio.

The vineyards and olive groves of Vathípetro

ÁYIOS NIKÓLAOS

Áyios Nikólaos is one of the busiest
tourist centres on Crete and, though
tourism has swamped most traces of
Cretan character, the town is still well
worth a visit.

Mirabéllo Bay (Kolpos Mirambellou)

Áyios Nikólaos sits on Mirabéllo Bay, the
Bay of the Beautiful View, so-named by
the Venetians who built a harbour here
in the 13th century. Well protected from
the prevailing westerly winds, the mirror-
like surface of the bay contributes to the
town's appeal, and there is a long
waterfront promenade running north
from the harbour along which to stroll
and enjoy the seaward views.

Lake Voulisméni

Right in the heart of the town is another
stretch of water – the almost perfectly
circular Lake Voulisméni, surrounded on
its western side by high creeper-clad
cliffs, and on its eastern side by
pavement cafés positioned to take
advantage of the lake views. So deep is
the lake in proportion to its
circumference that it was once thought
to be bottomless. In fact, it is now known
to be 64m deep at the centre, with
steeply sloping sides. Small boats can
now pass between the lake and the open
sea thanks to a channel dug in 1867–71.

Alongside this channel is the town's
original harbour where glass-bottomed
boats and luxury motor cruisers offer
trips to Spinalónga Island (see page 74)
or night-time tours of the bay with
dinner and Greek dancing. Running
southwest from the harbour are the
town's principal shopping streets, Odós
28 Octóbriou and Odós Koundoúrou
(see page 151).

On the waterfront: cafés line the circular 'bottomless' Lake Voulisméni

hair. She is less appealing than the delicate vessels made from marble and other coloured stones displayed in the same room.

Room 3 contains an exquisite stone libation vessel shaped like a triton shell. Carving such a vessel, using only primitive drills and abrasives, must have required exceptional skill and years of patient effort. The spirals of the outside of the shell are exactly duplicated on the inside of the vessel and the whole surface is decorated with a scarcely visible relief of daemons making a libation.

After this masterpiece of Minoan art, the Dedalic-style figurines of later rooms, clearly influenced by Egyptian art, seem crude and mass-produced, though the last room contains a macabre surprise – the grinning skull of a long-dead Roman with a funeral wreath of gold olive leaves garlanding his cranium. The skull came from a large Roman cemetery on the edge of Áyios Nikólaos. Placed in the mouth of the deceased was a 1st-century AD silver coin; such coins were traditionally placed in the mouth to pay the ferryman who, in Roman mythology, conveyed the dead to Hades across the River Styx.

Archaeological Museum

The town's archaeological museum is out of the centre, on the steep Odós Paleológou. Here, the origins of Minoan culture are particularly well represented, with good examples of neolithic and pre-palatial Minoan material on display in Room 1. Note the elegantly burnished vases with their long spouts and the stone phallus-shaped idol from a remote cave in Eastern Crete. The fertility theme continues in Room 2 where the so-called Goddess of Mýrtos is displayed, a bizarre early Minoan clay libation vase with phallic neck and head, clay lumps for breasts and a hatched triangle of pubic

A coin to pay the ferryman and a garland for the dead

Archaeological Museum: open Tuesday to Sunday, 8.30am–3pm; closed Monday. Admission charge).

Áyios Nikólaos is 70km east of Iráklio.

FAISTÓS AND AYÍA TRIÁDHA

At the same time as Arthur Evans was excavating Knosós in 1900, an Italian team was busy uncovering the equally extensive remains of the Minoan palace at Faistós. Evans' flair for self-publicity ensured that Knosós is now known the world over; far fewer people visit Faistós. This magnificently sited palace is set on the flanks of a hill jutting out into the rich agricultural Mesarás plain. Archaeologists have argued convincingly that the palace was deliberately oriented so as to make the most of the views, and there is evidence here for gardens and water cascades, all of which must have contributed to the pleasure of living in such a fine spot.

Site tour

Unlike Knosós, Faistós has not been reconstructed, and at first sight is rather confusing. Descending the path and steps

from the ticket office, the palace lies to the left (east) while the jumble of walls, wells and circular storage pits to the right belong to the Minoan town that clustered round the palace and cascaded down the slope of the hill to the plain below.

The West Court

The path brings you down to the West Court (1), with its raised footpath. From here there are good views of the imposing west façade of the palace (3), aligned to face the setting sun. In fact, two façades are visible: the monumental staircase on the left and the massive walls to either side of it belong to the New Palace, built after the earthquake of 1700BC. Running along the eastern edge of the West Court is the massive step-like plinth of the Old Palace façade, built around 1900BC. Standing in the West Court it is clear that the remains of the Old Palace were levelled to create a platform on which the New Palace was erected. Archaeologists are still working on the southern part of the site to uncover more of the Old Palace and its associated town connected by a well-paved road.

It is probable that valuable commodities, such as oil and grain, were carried in procession up this road to the palace, then brought up the monumental staircase(6) to the palace storerooms (9).

The Monumental Staircase

The staircase leads to a lobby marked by the base of a massive circular pillar (7). Beyond the lobby are the remains of a triple-pillared entrance (8) to a courtyard, or lightwell (a room open to the sky), from which narrow and winding passages lead left into the palace apartments and right into a massive stores complex (9).

Left: looking down to the West Court
Right: carved masonry, perhaps for a game

FAISTÓS SITE PLAN

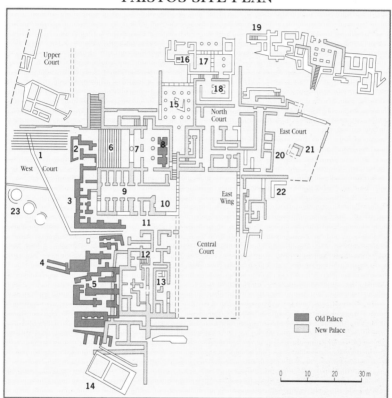

Key to the map

1 Theatre area
2 Shrine complex
3 West façade
4 Ramp
5 Shops
6 Grand stairway
7 Propylaeum
8 Lightwell
9 Storeroom block
10 Pillared hall
11 Corridor
12 Lustral basin
13 Pillar crypt
14 Temple of Rhea
15 Peristyle hall
16 Lustral basin
17 King's apartments
18 Queen's apartments
19 Archives
20 Workshops
21 Furnace
22 Colonnaded court
23 Storage pits
    (cisterns)

Storage and distribution

Grain and oil were stored in large jars within the palace stores complex, the doors fastened with rope or cord to which a clay seal was attached to indicate ownership. Archaeologists found over 300 different seals, with designs ranging from animals to battle scenes and portraits. It is still not clear precisely how the Minoan economy worked, but the palace played an important role in the storage of valuable commodities – and perhaps in their distribution as well. It is possible that Minoans paid tax in the form of oil and grain – or that the ruling family was regarded as the owner of all the oil and grain produced by the community, or that individual owners entrusted their commodities to the palace for safekeeping.

Symbol of wealth: oil storage jar

Central Court

The stores complex runs along the west flank of the large Central Court, aligned to make the most of northward views to Mount Ida – and specifically to the cave at Kamáres, which was an important focus of religious ritual during the Minoan era. To the north of the court, the narrow entrance to the private palace apartments is flanked by sentry boxes. This corridor was open to the sky – hence the drainage channel to carry rainwater away. The corridor leads to the North Court, to the right of which was a small walled garden. To the north of the court, a double room (17) also gave views – again to Mount Ida. Leading from this room, down to the right, is a series of structures relating to the Old Palace, in one of which the famous and mysterious Faistós disc (now in the Archaeological Museum, Iráklio), was found. The disc, of baked clay, is covered in indecipherable hieroglyphs arranged in a spiral pattern, perhaps having some religious significance.
Faistós is open Monday to Saturday, 8am–5pm and Sunday 9am–3pm. Admission charge.

AYÍA TRIÁDHA

On the West side of the same hill on which Faistós sits there is another important Minoan site, Ayía Triádha, traditionally described as a royal villa (for details of how to get there, see page 89). Archaeologists are still not sure of the precise role of this building, or its relationship to Faistós. It has been described as a rural retreat for the use of the Faistós ruling family, and the very fine frescos found here reinforce the idea that that this was a place of leisured

Ayía Triádha: perhaps a summer palace or a cultural centre for sport, dance and song

luxury. Also found here were the Chieftain Cup, Boxer Rhyton and Harvester Vase, the three famous stone vases now in the Archaeological Museum, Iráklio (see page 32).

The idyllic setting of the villa adds to the notion that it was built for pleasure, for the building sits on a slope with views towards the glistening Mesará Bay (Kolpos Mesaras). It may once have stood even closer to the sea, for there is evidence to suggest that waves once lapped the base of the hill; silt deposition has pushed the sea back considerably over the last three to four millennia.

Site tour

Since the Minoan name of the villa is not known, Ayía Triádha is named after a nearby church – but oddly enough, not the one that actually stands on the site: this church, ÁyiosYeóryios, nevertheless makes a good viewpoint from which to understand the site. Looking from the apse north to Mount Ida, the villa lies below, partly roofed over as a protection against rain. To the left are the private

apartments, in the middle the storage areas and to the right the public rooms for entertainment and ceremonies.

Beyond the villa is the main street of a small town. Shops, all identical in size and shape, line the right-hand side of the street, fronted by a row of column bases which once supported a colonnade, perhaps to shelter market stalls. The presence of these shops so close to the villa is one reason for questioning the theory that it was a royal residence. Perhaps the whole site was a centre for large seasonal gatherings of some kind – for sport, ritual, song and dance, maybe? Only further excavation will reveal the truth. What is not in doubt is the ferocity of the fire that destroyed this building in 1450BC – fire-blackened floors and steps provide a vivid reminder of the final fate of the Minoan palace culture.

Ayía Triádha is open Monday to Saturday, 8.30am–3pm, Sunday 9.30am–2.30pm. Admission charge.

Faistós and Ayía Triádha are 64km southwest of Iráklio.

GÓRTINA

When the Romans conquered Crete in 67BC, the people of Górtina took the side of the Roman general, Quintus Metellus. As a reward, their city was made capital of the Roman province of Cyrenaica, which also encompassed parts of north Africa. By the time of the Roman conquest, Górtina was already an ancient city, described by the ancient Greek historian, Strabo, as having a wall 10km in diameter. It was comprehensively remodelled along typical Roman lines, with baths, theatres, a governor's palace and a forum. The site today is massive, but only a fraction has been excavated. The Roman remains lie scattered across a huge area, with fallen columns lying among vineyards and olive groves, and Roman brick and tile littering the ground. After Saracen raiders looted Górtina in AD824 it was simply abandoned and left to decay because of the difficulty of defending the site.

Church of St Titus

One building stands remarkably intact: the church of St Titus dominates the entrance to the site with its massive apse standing to the roof. The church dates back to the 6th century and is, by popular belief, the burial place of St Titus, the first bishop of Crete. Titus was sent here on a successful mission to convert Crete to Christianity after St Paul had visited the island in AD50. It is quite likely that Titus would have made Górtina his base, since it was then the largest city on Crete, with a population of 30,000.

The Law Code of Górtina

Emerging from what would have been the west door of the church of St Titus, you can see, over to the right, the impressive remains of the 1st-century BC Odeon, a theatre built for music and poetry recitals. The modern brick structure to the rear of the theatre shelters a remarkable 10m stretch of wall covered in ancient Greek

script, recording the Laws of Górtina. Much of what we know about early Greek life and society comes from this important document, carved in sandstone and found among the foundations of a pre-Roman building on the site of the Odeon.

The inscription reads from left to right and from right to left on alternate lines, in a style known as *boustrophedon*, meaning 'like the pattern made by oxen ploughing a field'. Though the inscription dates to around 450BC, it probably records laws that had been observed for generations before – indeed, Plato, who mentions the code in his own book of Laws, describes it as very conservative code. It divides the inhabitants of Górtina into four classes – rulers, freemen, serfs and slaves – and describes in detail the rights of each with regard to property ownership, inheritance, marriage, divorce and the adoption of children, as well as laying down appropriate penalties for crimes such as rape, adultery and assault.

Temples and palaces

More excavated remains lie on the opposite side of the road. Turn left (east) along the Iráklio road and walk for some 300m, ignoring the right turn to Mitrópoli/Léndas. Look for a paved track on the right-hand side of the road which leads down to the Temple of Isis and Serapis, built in the 1st century AD for the worship of these Egyptian gods. To the south is the Temple of Apollo Pythios, a fascinating structure which may have been constructed as early as the 7th century BC and which then served as the main temple of the Roman city.

A track skirts the massive palace complex of the Roman provincial governor – the ruler of Crete and much of North Africa, responsible for ensuring a steady flow of wheat from these territories to other parts of the Roman Empire. Through the site fence it is possible to see beautifully paved courtyards, headless statues, fallen columns and numerous walls.

Open: the area enclosing the church of St Titus and the Odeon is open Tuesday to Sunday, 8.30am–3pm, closed Monday. Admission charge. The rest of site lies in olive groves and can be explored at will. Górtina is 46km south of Iráklio and 16km east of Faistós.

The 7th-century BC Temple of Apollo Pythios, with its stepped altar (left) was superseded by Áyios Títos church (right) in the 6th century AD

Exploring the streets and houses of the Minoan town of Gourniá

GOURNIÁ

Gourniá is one of the best examples of an ancient Minoan town. It sits on a low hill near the safe anchorage of the Mirabello Bay and the finds from the site indicate that it was a thriving industrial centre involved in pottery, metalworking and carpentry.

Most of the visible remains date to the New Palace period (1700–1450BC), although there was a settlement here in the Old Palace period (from 1900BC). The houses of the village were once several storeys high, and the very substantial walls that remain represent the basements, used for storage and as workshops, rather than the living areas. Turning left as you enter the site, you will walk up one of the main streets of the town, with its original paving intact. The street curves to the right and climbs to a flat area known as the Town Court. To the left (north) of this are the massive walls of a palatial building that may have

been the residence of a local governor. The entrance to the palace site is marked by a flight of four steps. To the left of this is a huge stone slab, pierced by a hole in one corner. It has been suggested that this was an altar on which bulls were sacrificed; others have proposed that the slab was merely a butcher's block and that the Town Court served as a market place rather than as a ceremonial or sacrificial site.

Bearing left from the slab, walk downhill to the palace's massive sandstone east façade. Continuing down the path, ignore the first flight of stairs and take the second right which leads to a small shrine where cult objects associated with the Snake Goddess were found. From this point there is an excellent panorama of the whole site. *Gourniá is 90km east of Iráklio, 21km southeast of Áyios Nikólaos. Open: Tuesday to Sunday, 8.30am–3pm. Closed: Monday. Free.*

IERÁPETRA

Ierápetra stands at the southern tip of a narrow neck of land where the distance between the north and south coast is a mere 12km. There is little of interest on the broad flat plain to the north of Ierápetra, but wildflower lovers should look out for the entrance to the Monastiráki Gorge on the east of the road, a great cleft in the rock renowned for its plants. In Episkopí, 5km further south, an unusual 12th-century church lies almost hidden, below road level, opposite the unmissable, large modern church. Excavations have revealed that the church replaced an earlier one, perhaps 4th century in date, overlying a series of catacombs, or Early Christian burial chambers.

Ierápetra itself is the southernmost town in Europe, the biggest town on the south coast and a thriving tourist resort. Thanks to an earthquake that destroyed the town in 1780, there are few signs that this was once a major Mediterranean trading port, particularly under the Romans. Displays in the small archaeological museum (open erratic hours) merely hint at the richness of the ancient town; important exhibits are the Minoan clay coffin, painted with hunting scenes, and the 2nd-century AD statue of Demeter, Roman goddess of agriculture.

Down on the harbour, the Venetian fortress (*open daily, 9am–9pm; admission charge*) provides a more recent parallel for the earthquakes that destroyed the island's Minoan palaces in 1700BC. In this case, it was in 1780 that the fort collapsed as a result of a massive earthquake, killing 300 men of the garrison. Just up from the harbour, signposts point to a house in which it is claimed, (on very slim evidence) that Napoleon stayed one night in 1798,

during his Egyptian campaign.

From Ierápetra, it is possible to take the south coast road east to Sitiá, diverting after 21km on the dirt road to Moní Kapsá. The little-visited monastery of Moní Kapsá, founded in 1471, enjoys a spectacular coastal setting to the east of Ieráptera, and was largely rebuilt in the 19th century by Yerontoyiannis, a hermit who is revered locally as a saint, and whose body is preserved in a silver reliquary in the monastery church. *Ierápetra is 107km southeast of Iráklio, 36km south of Áyios Nikólaos.*

Ierápetra's Venetian harbourside fortress

Knosós

Knosós is one of the world's most famous archaeological sites and in high season it swarms with visitors. It is open for long hours and a visit over lunchtime or in the early evening may prove more enjoyable than a morning visit when the crowds are at their peak.

The present palace at Knosós is the last in a series of buildings on the site that date back to the origins of civilisation on Crete. Beneath the palace, archaeologists have discovered the remains of a neolithic settlement, dating to around 6000BC. The earliest palace on the site dates from around 2000BC. This, like all the other palaces on Crete, was destroyed in the earthquake of 1700BC and then rebuilt to take its present form.

Today, despite the collapse of the upper storeys of the palace, which were built of timber and mud brick, it is still possible to gauge something of its vast and labyrinthine nature. Only a fraction of the site is open to the public. At its height, the palace and its town spread over 75ha and had a population of around 12,000 – the same as Iráklio in the Middle Ages.

Continuity

Unlike the other palaces of Crete, Knosós was only partially damaged by fire in 1450BC; neither was it abandoned at that date – indeed, Knosós has been inhabited continuously ever since, and the present villages of Knosós and Makritíkhos lie on top of the Minoan town.

Even so, the site has been preserved in a remarkable state: wonderful treasures, such as the gaming board and the statue of the Snake Goddess, now in the Archaeological Museum in Iráklio,

along with bronze vessels, stone jars and the throne itself were all found where they had been left. This suggests that, for centuries after the end of Minoan civilisation, the site was respected and not robbed – perhaps because of powerful memories of the myth of the Minotaur, the bull-headed monster of the labyrinth, who was thought to dwell beneath the palace.

Site tour

Visitors to the site are greeted by a bust of Arthur Evans (see pages 58-9) who excavated Knosós between 1900 and 1906. The bust stands at the entrance to the West Court and, to the left, there are three huge stone-lined pits (1), probably built as granaries. At the base of the central pit you can see the steps and stone walls of one of the oldest stone houses found on the site, built around 2000BC.

West Court

The whole of the palace complex served a ceremonial purpose, and the raised paths that cross the West Court were built as processional ways. Follow the raised path to the right of the Court and you will come up to the roped-off palace façade, clad in huge blocks of gypsum. This light and easily carved stone was used throughout the palace for cladding and paving. The use of gypsum for the façade would have given the palace a gleaming white, marble-like apearance.

The restored North Entrance which originally displayed an imposing fresco of a Charging Bull

Corridor of the Procession Fresco

To the right of the façade is the West Porch (2), marked by a single central column base. Imagine now that massive double doors lie ahead. These swing open as we enter the Corridor of the Procession Fresco (3), so-called because the walls were lined on both sides with a frieze depicting hundreds of life-sized youths and maidens in procession and playing music.

The floor, still intact, is paved with sheets of blue schist set in red mortar. The corridor ends abruptly because the hillside has fallen away at this point; it once ran around three sides of a rectangle to return to the Central Court of the palace. To get there, turn left, then right through a reconstructed doorway into the paved area known as the South Propylaea (4). Here a copy of the Cup Bearer Fresco has been placed on the wall. Egyptian in style, this is the best preserved of the figures from the Procession Fresco. Looking back, note the tapered red painted wooden columns that support the reconstructed doorways of the palace. The Minoans used whole trees as pillars, but inverted them, so that the wider root end of the tress was at the top.

Upper Propylaea

Beyond the fresco, the staircase ahead (5) leads to an area of the palace completely reconstructed by the excavator, Arthur Evans. It was his theory that the main reception rooms of

Key to map

 1 Walled pits
 2 West porch
 3 Corridor of the procession fresco
 4 South propylaeum
 5 Staircase to piano nobile
 6 Lower storeroom block
 7 Pillar crypts
 8 Room of the column bases
 9 Room of the tall pithos
10 Temple repository
11 Vat room
12 Antechamber
13 Throne room
14 Inner sanctuary
15 Lower long corridor
16 Deposit of tablets
17 Lustral basin
18 Royal road
19 Theatre area
20 Old keep
21 Northwest portico
22 North entrance passage
23 Pillar hall
24 Corridor of the draughts board
25 Northeast hall
26 Magazines of giant pithoi
27 East bastion
28 Court of the stork spout
29 Craftsman's workshop
30 East portico
31 Magazine of the medallion pithoi
32 Corridor of the bays
33 East–west corridor
34 Grand staircase
35 Hall of the colonnades
36 Hall of the double axes
   (King's megaron)
37 Queen's megaron
38 Bathroom
39 Toilet
40 Court of the distaffs
41 Shrine of the double axes
42 Corridor of sword tablets
43 House of chancel screen
44 Minoan kiln
45 House of the fallen blocks
46 House of sacrificed oxen

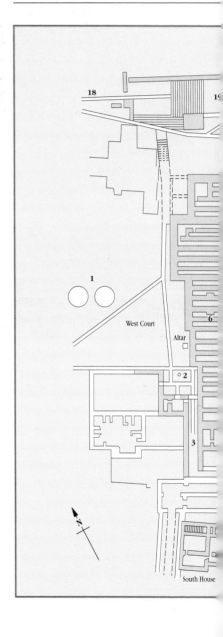

KNOSÓS SITE PLAN

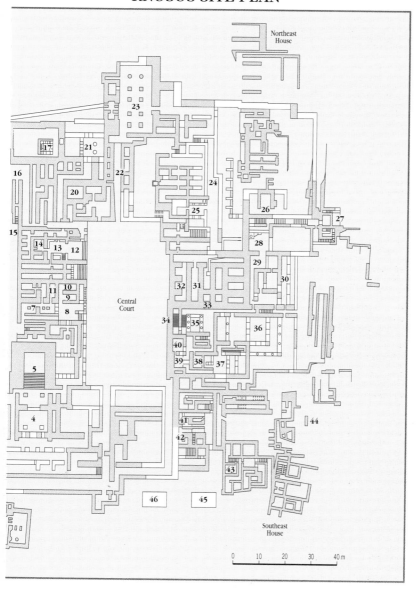

Northeast House

Central Court

Southeast House

0   10   20   30   40 m

The Central Court, with the Throne Room beyond, was the ritual centre of palace life

the palace lay on this well-lit and airy upper storey. As you cross the upper floor, there are views to the left down onto the palace storerooms. Here you can see clearly the *pithoi*, giant storage jars, lining the long walls of each room, and then cisterns dug into the floor of the central corridor to create more storage space. We know, from Linear B clay tablets, that oil, grain, wool, dyestuffs and textiles were stored in rooms such as these, representing very considerable wealth.

Straight ahead lies a gallery where reproductions of the most famous Knosós frescos have been hung, and through this room you reach a terrace. Turn left and left again to find a little staircase – one of many that must have provided a short cut from one part of the labyrinthine palace to another. Of equal interest is the fact that the walls containing the staircase are built on foundations from the Old Palace – hence its unusual rounded shape.

Central Court and Throne Room
The staircase brings you down to the Central Court, with the palace Throne Room on the right. In the antechamber (12) is a reconstruction of what Evans called 'the oldest throne in the world' – whilst the original gypsum throne

survives intact, standing where it was placed some 3,500 years ago, in the railed off inner sanctum (13). This Throne Room was in disarray when Evans excavated it, with jars overturned and littering the floor – enough for him to suggest that some dramatic final event took place here.

Royal Apartments
On the opposite side of the Central Court are the Royal Apartments (currently under restoration and likely to be closed to visitors). This suite contains the most gracious rooms in the palace, many of them decorated with fine frescos, such as the Dolphin, and the Girl Dancer Frescos. Originally reconstructed by Evans as bedrooms, bathrooms and dressing rooms, it is now thought more likely that they were shrines, and not domestic rooms of any sort at all.

Waterworks and gardens
Continuing to the north of the site, there is a roofed-over area known as the Magazine of the Giant Pithoi (26) part of the name of the room dating to the Old Palace period, and therefore almost 4,000 years old. Just in front of the magazine, steps descend right down to the palace east entrance. Lining the

staircase is a little water channel, with miniature rills (furrows to make the water ripple as it flows) and cascades. Anyone entering the palace on this side would have been greeted by the gentle sound of running water. Returning past the giant *pithoi*, to the top of the steps straight ahead, you reach a paved area with floor grilles: here are terracotta pipes from the original palace water supply, and stone drainage channels to carry rainwater away. A covered room to the left is known as the Medallion Room (31) because of the medallion-like circles

Stucco bull's head (right) and *pithoi* (below) in the palace storerooms

applied as decoration to the giant storage jars found here. A staircase alongside brings you back to the Central Court.

Charging bulls and lustral basins

The north side of the Central Court is dominated by the imposing reproduction of the Charging Bull Fresco (22). Anyone entering the palace from the north side would have been greeted by this intimidating fresco, thought to have been part of a larger bull-leaping frieze. To the west of this is a reconstructed lustral basin (17), consisting of steps leading down to an area where visitors were expected to wash and anoint themselves with oil.

The Theatral Area

Going west again is an area enclosed on two sides by steps (19). These have been interpreted as seating for the audience at some kind of sport or ritual but alternative theories abound – more plausible is the idea that important guests were greeted here and, perhaps, entertained, before proceeding to the lustral basin for anointing and washing and then going on into the palace. Such an explanation fits with the fact that the Theatral Area stands at the end of the so-called Royal Road (18), a wide and well-paved street that connects the palace with the vast town that once surrounded it.

Knosós is 5km south of Iráklio. Open: in summer, Monday to Friday, 8am–6pm, Saturday, Sunday and public holidays, 8.30am–3pm; in winter, 10am–sunset daily. Admission charge.

ARTHUR EVANS

A bust of Sir Arthur John Evans (1851–1941) features prominently at the entrance to Knosós, paying tribute to a man who is something of a hero to the Cretans, as he should be, given how much Knosós earns in tourist revenue. Evans is less of a hero to the archaeological establishment, criticised for his intuitive reconstruction of frescos and rooms in the palace: Logan Pearsall Smith in a letter to Bernhard Berenson, wrote in 1926 that 'Evans is repainting and reconstructing

Evans' bust at Knosós, and finds from the palace

Knosós in a gaudy style of bad taste which gives it something of the look of his hideous house in Boar's Hill'.

Controversial figure

Few visitors today would agree with this harsh judgement, but it remains fashionable to find fault with Evans' theories and interpretations, just as it was in his own time.

Evans sometimes invited criticism because of his own strength of

character and his possessive attitude to all things Minoan. He was, after all, the owner of Knosós, having purchased the site in 1894, and used his own private fortune to fund the excavations. Ownership of the site was conveyed to the British School at Athens in 1924, and was then transferred to the Greek government in 1952.

many scholars. Linear A was in use from around 1650BC but was superseded, after the final destruction of the New Palaces in 1450BC, by the Mycenaean influenced Linear B – a script that has been deciphered in part, yielding a great deal of information about the Minoan economy, but, at a time when Minoan civilisation was a shadow of its former glory.

The discovery of the Minoans

Evans began digging in 1900, making sensational discoveries almost every day, discoveries that were reported with astonishment in newspapers all over Europe, as the history of the ancient world was completely rewritten.

Linear A and B

Evans' name has become inextricably linked with the Minoans but many other archaeologists have worked on the island, and continue to do so. The palace of Zákros was only discovered in 1961 and several sites are under excavation now, including the peripheral areas at Knosós. This work has added immensely to our knowledge of the Minoans, but their language and script – known as Linear A – has not yet been deciphered, despite enormous efforts on the part of

Abiding mysteries

The other great unsolved mystery is the precise cause of the fires that destroyed the Minoan palaces in 1450BC. Evans' theory that the eruption of Théra, a whole half century earlier, caused the calamity is no longer believed. Many alternative theories exist, none of them borne out by the evidence – but there is increasing support for the idea that a major exodus occurred after 1450, with the Minoans, expert seafarers, fleeing their island and migrating all over Europe to found new cultures. The Etruscans of ancient Italy and the Philistines of ancient Palestine are among the peoples whose ceramics, jewellery and bronze-work bears a striking and intriguing similarity to that of the Minoans.

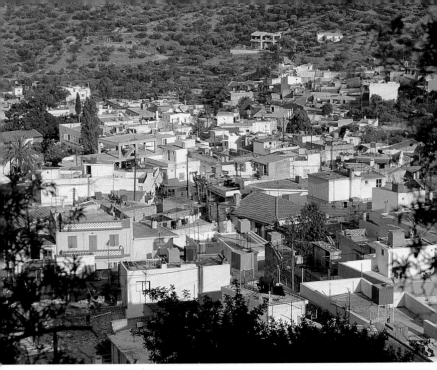

The densely packed houses of the hillside village of Kritsá

KRITSÁ

The church of Panayía Kerá (Our Lady of Kerá) stands on the right-hand (northern) side of the road just before the village of Kritsá, usually unmissable because of the large number of tour buses parked alongside. This tiny domed church is one of the most rewarding sights on Crete and by far the best on the island for Byzantine wall paintings.

The church has a complex chronology that begins with the construction of the central nave and apse in the mid-13th century, not long after the Venetian occupation of Crete. The earliest paintings are those of the apse, followed, at a slightly later date, by the paintings of the dome and nave. Next comes the south aisle (early 14th century) and finally the north aisle (mid-14th century). All the paintings have been cleaned and restored in recent years, and are remarkable for the vividness of their colour and the dramatic force of their composition.

The apse

The oldest paintings in the church are those of the apse. Here, the *Ascension*, on the ceiling, survives only as fragments, but Saints Nicholas, Chrysostom, Basil and Gregory, dressed in priestly vestments covered with crosses and holding scrolls, are depicted in fine and intricate detail around the walls; the furrowed brows of the saints, and their intense gaze, helps to convey the sense of exceptional wisdom and holiness, and to suggest that these holy men are absorbed in deep contemplation of the eternal mysteries.

The dome and nave

Next in date comes the dome, where four scenes from the Bible are illustrated: *Christ's Presentation in the Temple*, his *Baptism*, the *Raising of Lazarus* and his *Entry into Jerusalem on Palm Sunday*. Other scenes on the nave walls and vault include a charming Nativity and a gruesome *Massacre of the Innocents* on the south side. On the opposite side, the *Last Supper* shows a table set with fashionable Venetian glass. Another sign of Venetian influence is the very rare portrait, on the north wall, lower register (below St George), of St Francis of Assisi, a western, rather than an Orthodox, saint.

The south aisle

In the south aisle, an inscription names the donors of the fresco as the people of the village of Kritsá and one Antonios Lameras. The vibrant scenes depict the *Life of the Virgin* with an unusual degree of realism. In one scene, for example, Mary and Joseph sit dejected with their heads in their hands, obviously having had a row; Mary has just told Joseph of her pregnancy, and Joseph has misunderstood; a helpful angel is descending from heaven to intervene and allay Joseph's concerns about the Virgin's virtue. Another scene shows Joachim, dejected in the desert, fasting for 40 days in the hope that his barren wife, Anna, will conceive (note the shepherds with their stylish cocked hats). In the next scene, Joachim and Anna rush to embrace in a scene that beautifully expresses their joy at Anna's miraculous conception of a child who will prove to be the Virgin Mary.

The north aisle

The frescos here depict the Second Coming, with a vivid portrayal of the Garden of Paradise and its bird-filled trees and rivers. The first to be admitted to the garden by Saint Peter (bottom right) is the repentant thief who died with Christ on the cross. Seated with the Virgin and the Patriarchs are the Wise and Foolish Virgins of the Bible story, carrying candles and with resplendent jewellery and hairstyles. More sobre is the portrait of the donor on the opposite wall, with his wife and child, dressed in fine cloaks and linen caps in the style of the 14th century. Alongside, on the west wall, the Archangel Michael is blowing his trumpet to waken the dead and call them to Judgement – another angel weighs the resurrected souls in his scales. The earth is personified by a crowned female figure holding a snake that is coiled round her head – a throwback perhaps to the Minoan Snake Goddess? *Kritsá is 80km east of Iráklio, 10km southwest of Áyios Nikólaos. Open: daily 9.15am–3pm (to 2pm on Sunday). Admission charge.*

Panayía Kerá church, covered inside with glowing Byzantine frescos

Lasíthiou's canvas-sailed windmills draw water from underground reservoirs

The aquifers (underground reservoirs) are restocked by the heavy rains that fall from October onwards. Flooding would be a threat if it were not for the drainage channels that divide the plain up into a grid, resembling the squares on a chessboard. The drainage system was first installed by the Romans, but the present system, cleaned out and restored, was installed under Venetian rule.

Caves and farmhouses

Most visitors come to Lasíthiou for the Dhíktaen Cave at Psikhró (see page 70). A less crowded alternative is the Trapéza (or Krónio) cave, to the south of Tzermiadho. This was used for burials in the neolithic era (around 5000BC) and later as a Minoan sanctuary.

Also well worth a visit is the Folk Museum alongside the church in the village of Áyios Yeóryios. This occupies a genuine farmhouse, with low ceilings and smoke-blackened beams, built in 1800. Beside the door is a loom and the family bed is built over the wine press. Simple handmade furniture is stacked against the walls, and the kitchen area has a quern for grinding wheat, kneading troughs, a bread oven and storage jars for wine and olives.

Alongside is a byre for sheep and goats and a separate stable for donkeys, in which chickens roosted among the saddles, panniers and ploughs of the working farm. A more spacious and modern house alongside shows how Cretans live today.

Lasíthiou lies 60km southeast of Iráklio, 21km south of Mália. Folk Museum open daily 10am–6pm.

LASÍTHIOU

The Lasíthiou, also known as the Lasíthi Plain, is a large oval plateau, completely ringed by mountains, with some 17 small villages dotted around its rim. The villagers make their living from agriculture: apples, almonds and potatoes are the principal crops, and the plain is beautiful in spring when the fruit trees are in blossom. In summer, the fields are irrigated using hundreds of white-sailed windmills which draw water up from underground aquifers (for a suggested route, see page 86). The windmills are a famous and picturesque tourist attraction, though it can be hit and miss whether any will be operating at the time of your visit.

LATÓ

From Kritsá (see page 60) it is a short drive to the site of ancient Lató. On entering Kritsá, follow the one-way traffic system to the right. On a bend, after 300m, a sign points right to the archaeological site. From here, a metalled road passes 3.5km through ancient olive groves to the site car park.

The site

Lató is a relatively late foundation for Crete, dating from the Archaic period (7th century BC), after the end of mainstream Minoan culture. As always, wild flowers and splendid views add to the interest of the site. As you enter the site gate, a red arrow on the rocks points you up and to the right along a pottery-strewn track to the imposing city gate, built of massive square blocks of solidified lava. A tiny entrance, just wide enough to allow one person through, shows that no invader could enter the city from this direction without the greatest of difficulty.

The *Agora*

Beyond, the stepped main street leads between the walls of shops and workshops up to the *agora* (market place) at the top of the hill. From here, and from the theatre terrace to the right, there are almost limitless views of eastern Crete, showing why this hilltop had such a strategic value. The deep cistern nearby indicates too the importance of a water supply in the event of a seige.

To the left, on a higher terrace, are the remains of civic buildings where the town archives were kept and where a perpetual flame was kept alight as a symbol of the town's continuity and as an offering to Hestia, the ancient Greek goddess of the hearth.

Lató is 80km east of Iráklio, 10km south west of Áyios Nikólaos and 3.5km north of Kritsá. Open: Tuesday to Sunday, 8.30am–3pm. Closed Monday. Free.

Stone benches surround the hearths where fires burned in honour of the goddess Hestia

MÁLIA

Mália is the capital of beach-holiday Crete, a small town that has been swamped by discos, bars, English-style pubs and tavernas that sell beefburgers rather than Cretan food. The reason for all this development is the fine sandy beach that spreads for some distance either side of the town. Despite its size, this beach can be very crowded, and there are more atmospheric places to swim, one of them being just 4km east of Mália, alongside the Minoan palace remains. To the disco-hungry crowd who come to Mália, the fact that there is a major Minoan palace on the town's doorstep is probably a matter of supreme indifference, which helps to explain why

Sun worshippers enjoying the sandy beaches that stretch both sides of Mália

so few people visit the excavated remains and beach nearby.

The site

The palace sits on the coastal plain within sight and sound of the sea, and bumps in the fields to the south indicate the presence of a large town, as yet little explored. French-run excavations are continuing, and informative displays are found at key points around the site, explaining the work in progress.

A striking feature of the palace is the sheer number of areas set aside for storage. Sunken clay-lined pits and barrack-like blocks, built from mud brick and with their wine and oil-storage jars intact, surround the central court, leaving only a small area designated as living accommodation. To the northwest of the palace (in the area known as Quartier M),

archaeologists have uncovered a group of buildings used as the palace administration block. Clay tablets inscribed with inventorial data, and seal stones used to seal boxes, jars and doorways, have been found here in great quantity. As with other Minoan palace sites, the building clearly played a key role in the storage and distribution of goods, but we are no nearer to knowing whether Minoan society was authoritarian, with all resources owned and controlled by the ruling family, or whether it was based on a more benign system of communal ownership.

Mália is 38km east of Iráklio; Palace open Tuesday to Sunday, 8.30am–3pm; closed Monday; admission charge.

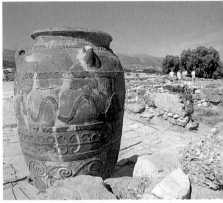

The palace site at Mália where you can watch excavations in progress

Nearby:
Mílatos

This attractive fishing village is set above a pretty pebble beach. Mílatos is mentioned by Homer as one of the Cretan towns that sent troops to fight in the Trojan War and archaeological evidence suggests that the village has been continually occupied for at least 5,000 years. Legend has it that migrants from this village founded the great and famous city of Miletos on the modern Turkish coast. Though this may seem no more than a coincidence of names, archaeologists have, in fact, found Minoan settlement remains at Turkish Miletos. Here in Cretan Mílatos, however, there is little to see of the ancient past, though the beachside tavernas are well worth sampling for their fresh fish.

Mílatos is 10km east of Mália.

Cretan Open-Air Museum

The Cretan Open-Air Museum is located just off the National Highway to the west of Khersónisos, another busy package-tour resort, some 12km to the west of Mália. Guided tours take in reconstructed Cretan houses, a chapel, windmill, shepherd's shelter, pottery and weaving workshops and an olive-oil press. Wine tastings and an audio-visual introduction to the attractions of Crete are all part of the package.

Cretan Open-Air Museum open Tuesday to Sunday 9.30am–2pm, closed Monday. Admission charge.

Káto Karouzaná

Káto Karouzaná bills itself as 'The Traditional Village'. Popular with coach tours, the village is really an excuse to persuade visitors to part with their money in return for handicrafts such as woven rugs and pottery (although handwoven and painted, the designs are not always traditional). Displays of Greek dancing and music are put on in the evening, and if you decide to book on a Cretan Evening tour, it is quite likely that you will be brought to this village for dinner and entertainment.

Káto Karouzaná lies 15km south of Khersónisos.

MÁTALA

Even if you are not a beach lover, Mátala's sheltered bay, sandstone cliffs and lovely sunset views will not leave you unmoved. Mátala also makes an excellent base for exploring the major archaeological sites of Faistós and Górtina. The beach is impeccably clean and local shops are very well stocked, as befits a village that has almost become a German colony (there are even fragments of the Berlin Wall hanging in the reception area of one hotel).

Archaeology

The cliffs to the north of the bay contain scores of man-made caves where hippies made their homes when Crete was first 'discovered' in the 1970s. The caves were originally excavated in the 2nd century BC to serve as rock-cut tombs, and some have ornate carved niches within. Today the caves are fenced off and out of bounds; archaeologists are busy recording the surviving features and working out how to prevent their further erosion.

A little to the north of Mátala is another fine sandy beach, stretching south from Kalamáki to Kómmos. Kómmos is the site of the Minoan harbour that served Faistós, and American archaeologists digging here in the last ten years have uncovered substantial remains of roads, warehouses, dry docks and temples, some of which can be seen through the site fence. *Mátala is 70km southwest of Iráklio, 10km southwest of Faistós.*

MIRTÍA

Níkos Kazantzákis is one of the few Cretans whose name is well known beyond the shores of his own island, though his fame owes much more to film versions of his work than to his actual writings. The Kazantzákis museum in Mirtía attempts to fill out the very vague picture that most of us have about his life and work. The museum is located on the village square in what is claimed to be the house of Kazantzákis' father. In fact it has been substantially extended to accommodate case after case of Kazantzákis memorabilia: books, stills from film and stage versions of his works, costume designs and personal possessions, such as his signet rings and fountain pens.

Kazantzákis (1883–1957) was born in Iráklio and studied law at Athens University and political science in Paris. Fellow Cretan Elifthérios Venizélos (see page 98) made Kazantzákis Minister of Welfare in his Greek government of 1919, but he preferred travelling to politics, and lived abroad for many years

The striking rock-cut tombs of Mátala were also used as homes in the past

Mátala's west-facing bay is the place to watch the sun go down

CRETAN LIARS

On the way up to Mirtía look out for the distinctive profile of Mount Yioúktas to the west (right) once past Knosós. The mountain, with its radar station, looks like a human face, with prominent brow, nose, lips and chin. Cretans have long believed that this is the face of Zeus who lies buried beneath the mountain. Other Greeks branded Cretans as liars for daring to suggest that Zeus was anything but immortal (see page 71).

whilst writing a series of poems, plays, stories and poetic dramas. His grandiose language is out of fashion now, and his work is little read or performed.

Controversy

Kazantzákis became widely known through the enormous success of *Zorba the Greek* (1946), which was turned into a popular film with a haunting theme tune starring Anthony Quinn and Alan Bates (1964). Controversy also helped to promote his name: *Freedom or Death* (1953), about the Cretan resistance to Turkish rule, and *The Last Temptation of Christ* (1954) were both condemned by the Roman Catholic church for blasphemy. More recently, Martin Scorsese's film version of *The Last Temptation of Christ* ran into similar trouble, criticised for portraying Christ as flawed and truly human, rather than sinless and divine. Conspiracy theorists claim that the Church prevented Kazantzákis from receiving the Nobel Prize for Literature when he was nominated in 1955; the truth is that there was an infinitely better candidate called Albert Camus.

Mirtia is 32km southeast of Iráklio, 20km southeast of Knosós. Open: daily 9am–6pm.

MONÍ TOPLÓU

Moní Toplóu, or Toplóu
monastery, sits on top of a
bleak and windswept rocky
plateau at the northeastern
tip of the island, where few
other people live. Toplóu
is a word of Turkish origin
meaning 'armed with
cannon' and the monastery
has been plundered and
destroyed several times,
hence its fortress-like
appearance today. The
monastery is immensely
wealthy and the monks
have restored much of the
complex (critics say they
have destroyed its
character in the process) including a fine
old Cretan windmill that stands just
outside the monastery walls. This
survives with its internal workings intact,
providing a rare opportunity to see how
the canvas sails turned the giant
millstones within.

Fortress-like Moní Toplóu and
its pretty wheel window

The ancient monastic
complex

The gatehouse of the
ancient part of the
monastery leads into a
delightful shady patio,
paved with cobbles. Three
storeys of monastic cells
surround the courtyard on
three sides, with a tall
belltower, rising above the
gatehouse, filling the
fourth side. The tiny
church to the right has a
pretty wheel window and
four panels set into the
façade. One is carved with a Virgin and
Child in relief, dating perhaps to the
14th century when the church monastery
was founded. Two other panels have
inscriptions recording the restoration of
the church after the 1612 earthquake.
The fourth panel, a grey slab covered in

minute script, dates from 132BC and records the so-called 'Arbitration of Magnesia'. The rulers of the city of Magnesia (now in western Turkey) were called in to arbitrate in a long-standing land dispute between Ítanos (see below) and Ierápetra. The judgement (which came down in favour of Ítanos) was recorded on this slab and on a matching slab that still survives in Magnesia. Long after the dispute was forgotten, the slab was reused, first as a grave marker, then as an altar; its importance was not appreciated until a 19th-century Classics scholar, Robert Pashley, came across it when visiting this monastery in 1834.

Icons and engravings

The church contains a magnificent icon, called *Lord, thou art Great* because each of the 61 tiny scenes packed into the painting illustrate a line from this Greek Orthodox prayer. The scenes sum up the whole Biblical story, from Creation to the Last Judgement, with especially lively depictions of the Story of Noah, Jonah and the Whale and the Destruction of the Cities of the Plain. A museum to the rear of the church contains more icons, but none as riveting as this one.

A further museum across the courtyard is devoted to 19th-century engravings of Mount Athos, once made by the monks to sell as souvenirs. These are of limited interest, but do look for the tiny room to one side of the museum devoted to the monastery's role in the Cretan struggle for independence against the Turks and during World War II, when the abbot was executed for assisting the Resistance.

Moní Toplóu is 150km east of Iráklio, 14km east of Sitiá. Open: daily 9am–1pm and 1.15–5pm. Admission charge.

Nearby:
Palm Beach

From Moní Toplóu a scenic road runs north through a bare upland landscape populated only by hardy sheep and goats. Just when you have convinced yourself that nothing could grow here except the most hardy of shrubs, you encounter beautiful groves of date palms at Vái. These are a distinct species of palm, known only on eastern Crete, and recorded as early as Roman times. They have given their name to the so-called Palm Beach at Vái, a lovely, but often very crowded, stretch of white sand. Just 2km to the north are the excavated ruins of the hilltop city of Ítanos, once an important harbour involved in trade with Egypt and the Near East.

Another important archaeological site is the ancient Minoan town Palaíkastro, some 8km south of Vái. There is little to see here at present, but recent field surveys suggest that the town was second only in size to that at Knosós, with the potential to yield much information about life for ordinary people in Minoan Crete.

Palm Beach is rarely so uncrowded

PSIKHRÓ AND THE DHÍKTAEN CAVE

The great god Zeus, destined to become the supreme deity and ruler of the heavens, was born in the Dhíktaen Cave at some time back in the mists of antiquity (see page 34). Today, that cave is one of the major tourist attractions on Crete but it is difficult to find awe and reverence among the crowds who throng the cave.

Practicalities

The cave entrance lies above the village of Psikhró, a village almost entirely given over to the feeding of coach-borne visitors to the cave and to the sale of souvenirs. The cave entrance is a steep 15-minute climb up a well-trodden path. You can travel up on the back of a donkey, in true Cretan peasant style, if you prefer.

This is one of the few places on Crete where you are likely to encounter heavy sales technique. Hawkers pester visitors with offers of guided tours and you may even be told that hiring a guide is compulsory: it is not, and it is entirely up to you whether you want someone to accompany you and point out the principal features of the cave.

The cave itself echoes to the anxious chatter of ill-equipped visitors frightened that they are going to slip on the damp rock of the steeply descending cave footpath, or lose their way in the gloom. The lesson of all this is to come well-equipped – a torch is very useful, as are non-slip shoes and a sweater against the cold of the cave interior. You can enjoy a degree of privacy by coming early in the morning or in the late afternoon, avoiding the worst of the coach tours which congregate here in the hour or so before and after lunch.

The cave

The Dhíktaen Cave is located in the northern flanks of the Díkte mountain range (Órosira Dhíkti) at an altitude of 1,025m. The cave consists of a vast cavern, some 15m high and 85m deep. At the lowest section there is a small pool and a number of stalagmites that divide this part of the cave into a number of smaller chambers. Guides will tell you that the stalagmite column to the right of the pool represents Zeus's Mantle, and that it was here that the infant Zeus was fed by nymphs on wild honey and goat's milk, while the chamber to the left is where Zeus was born.

The same chamber is where, in 1899–1900, archaeologists found the greatest concentration of votive offerings, including bronze and clay figurines, gold brooches and bronze axes, miniature versions of the sacred Minoan *labrys*, or double-bladed axe. These offerings had

The view from the Dhíktaen Cave over the Lasíthiou Plain

Local guides have given fanciful names to the stalagmites in the Dhíktaen Cave

been thrown into the pool or placed in crevices and cracks around the cave wall and on the stalagmites. Most corresponded to the New Palace period on Crete (1600–1450BC), with another group of finds dating from the Iron Age (8th and 7th centuries BC), representing a revival in the use of the cave for religious ritual. Higher up in the cave, nearer to the entrance, libation tables and altars were found along with the bones of sacrificial animals.

The legend of Zeus

Like other large caves on Crete, this was regarded as a holy place. Whether or not it really is the cave referred to in ancient myth as the birthplace of Zeus is a subject still debated by scholars. Epimenides the poet, born on Crete sometime in the 6th or 7th centuries BC, at about the time when the cult of Zeus was being revived, felt inclined to disbelieve the claims of his own countrymen. Indeed, he was the poet who famously branded all Cretans as liars

(see page 67), adding that they were 'noxious beasts' and 'evil bellies'. St Paul was later to quote these same words in writing to his follower, Titus, who was sent to Crete to convert the islanders to Christianity around AD50. The reason for this violent disapproval was the Cretan belief that Zeus (regarded by all Greeks as immortal) was dead and lay buried beneath Mount Yioúktas (see page 67).

Cretans have a simple answer to this accusation: their Zeus is a different one from the Greek Zeus; the Cretan Zeus, worshipped as far back as neolithic times, was a vegetation god who died and rose again annually, rather than the Greek Zeus, the immortal sky god, who has attributes more in common with Oriental and Egyptian deities.

Psikhró is 62km southeast of Iráklio, on the southern rim of the Lasíthiou Plain. The Dhiktaen Cave lies 2km south of the village and is open Tuesday to Saturday, 8am–6pm and Sunday 10am–5pm. Closed: Monday. Admission charge.

Setting out from Sitiá to catch the fish served in the tranquil town's many tavernas

SITIÁ

Sitiá is the easternmost town of any significance on Crete. If you are interested in visiting this part of the island it makes a far more interesting base than Áyios Nikólaos or Ierápetra, having an easy-going but self-assured Cretan character, little affected by tourism. Tavernas are full of local people and the food is of noticeably better quality than in the major resorts. No visitor to Sitiá on a Sunday leaves without being impressed by the vitality of the evening stroll, the *voltá*, a legacy of Venetian rule, when just about everyone, old and young, priest and people, comes out to promenade along the palm-fringed seafront in their Sunday best. The town is worth a visit in August when the importance of the local raisin and sultana crop is celebrated with its Sultana Festival. This is one of the liveliest excuses for song, dance and over-consumption to be found on Crete.

The sights

Continuing along the seafront opposite the Star hotel are Roman semi-circular rock-cut fish tanks. They are not easy to spot, being below the water line at times, and were once used for storing live fish until they were needed. On the hill is the square Venetian fortress, dating from the 13th century and now partly restored to serve as an open-air theatre.

Both of Sitiá's museums are located on the fringes of the town. The Folklore Museum is in Odós Therissoú, on the road to Áyios Nikólaos, and is notable for its collection of woven rugs, bed-hangings and blankets. The Archaeological Museum is to be found in the unpromising location of an industrial estate on the Ieráptra road, sandwiched between a marble mason's yard and a graveyard for rusting and broken-down tractors.

Ancient querns and kneading trough at Praisós

Archaeological Museum

The museum is, nevertheless, well laid out and labelled. The star exhibit is a wonderful ivory statue of a Minoan youth, known as the Palaíkastro Kouros. This has been painstakingly pieced together from numerous scattered fragments. The fire-blackened ivory recalls the dramatic final events that took place on Crete in 1450BC when many Minoan towns and palaces were destroyed in an inferno.

Among the other exhibits are a number of extremely rare tablets covered in the as-yet undeciphered Linear A script (see page 59). Other rarities include a bronze carpenter's saw from Zákros, a clay wine press, and a clay barbecue grill. The final section of the museum contains Roman and Hellenistic material, including some fine bronze fish hooks, nails and jewellery.

Sitiá is 140km east of Iráklio, 70km east of Áyios Nikólaos. Folklore Museum open: April to October, Tuesday to Sunday, 9.30am–3.30pm; closed Monday; admission charge. Archaeological Museum open: daily 9am–1pm and 1.15–5pm. Admission charge Monday to Saturday.

Nearby:

Praisós

Some of the finds in the Sitiá Archaeological Museum come from the Hellenistic site of Praisós. This is worth seeking out, especially in spring, when it is carpeted in wildflowers. The site is known to have been a major town of the Etocretans mentioned by Homer, that is, the rump of the Minoan peoples who survived the conflagration of 1450BC and who continued with the old religious practices. Defensive works can be seen and one fully excavated 3rd-century BC house, with extant olive press, water cistern and mortar.

Praisós is 15km south of Sitiá.

NIKOS THE PELICAN

Along with visitors and townspeople, Nikos the Pelican is also to be found strolling about in the vicinity of the seafront, though you can never be quite sure where. Nikos is a much pampered, and now quite elderly, pelican who got himself caught up in a fisherman's net some years ago. Having been set free and fed, he decided to hang around the town.

SPINALÓNGA AND ELOÚNDHA

The tiny offshore island of Spinalónga makes a popular excursion from both Áyios Nikólaos and Eloúndha. In both cases, tours depart from the harbour at regular intervals during the day, and the round trip takes about four hours. There may be an opportunity to swim during the trip and refreshments are served on the larger boats – otherwise, be sure to take something to eat and drink with you.

Spinalónga peninsula

You will see Spinalónga peninsula on the right-hand side (east) of the boat if you are travelling from Eloúndha, and on the left of the boat travelling from Áyios Nikólaos. The peninsula is known locally as 'Big Spinalónga' to distinguish it from the island, and it is attached to Crete only by a narrow sandspit. There is little to see here now of the once-thriving Hellenistic and Roman port of Oloús that stood at the southern end of the peninsula.

Spinalónga island

Spinalónga (which means 'Long Thorn' in Italian, a reference to its shape and pointed profile) is noted for having one of Crete's finest and best-preserved Venetian fortresses, built here in 1579

The view to Spinalónga's fortress (left) and from the fortress to Eloúndha (below)

to protect the approaches to Spinalónga bay and the Gulf of Mirabello. Remarkably, it remained in Venetian hands long after the rest of Crete fell to the Turks in 1669, following the 22-year siege of Iráklio. Spinalónga was only surrendered to the Turks in 1715, and for several decades before that it was a place of refuge for Cretan resistance fighters and for Christians escaping forcible conversion to Islam.

After 1715, Turkish families were settled on the island to prevent its use as a safe haven by Cretans. When the Turkish occupation ended at the end of the 19th century, the island was abandoned. From 1903 to 1955 it was used as a colony – in effect a prison – for lepers and others suffering from contagious diseases, a cruel and unnecessary practice. The island's lepers made what kind of a life they could among the ruins of the Turkish village, which remains a major feature of the island to this day, albeit in a state of advanced decay.

Eloúndha beach, a quieter spot than the nearby resort of Áyios Nikólaos

Eloúndha

Eloúndha village has developed into a small and charming resort built around a harbour where fishermen can often be seen sorting and cleaning their catch and repairing their nets. Some visitors to eastern Crete prefer this quieter resort to the bustle of Áyios Nikólaos further south. To the south of the town, signposts pointing to 'The Other Side of Eloúnda' (*sic*) direct you down a long causeway to Spinalónga peninsula, with its walks, bird life and fine coastal views.

Magnificent views over the Gulf of Mirabello are also to be had from the hills surrounding the town, especially on the winding road west, signposted to Neápoli, which leads to the hilltop site of ancient Dréros. Here the remains of an *agora* (market place) and public buildings can be made out, including the footings of an 8th-century BC temple to Apollo Delphinios: though they may not look much, these remains represent one of the very first classical temples ever built in Greece, and are therefore of great archaelogical importance.

Eloúndha is 72km east of Iráklio, 12km north of Áyios Nikólaos.

The church at Vorí: most visitors to the village make for the adjacent museum

Food from the wild

The displays here will answer a lot of the questions that any inquisitive traveller on Crete will have at the back of their minds. For example, what are the plants that the little old ladies, clad in black, are foraging for when you see them scouring the wild rocky hillsides of Crete. Case Number 1 provides some answers and covers the theme of foods gathered in the wild, from freshwater crabs and snails, to wild 'greens' (*horta* in Greek) – plants picked from the hillsides at any time from autumn until late spring and cooked by boiling, or frying in oil. The ingredients of *horta* include many relatives of the dandelion, as well as wild asparagus and artichoke. Once, such wild foods were a vital supplement to a near-starvation diet – today they are soul food for Cretans, evoking memories of the simple life of their forefathers, and the little old ladies make a substantial income from selling the results of their foraging in local markets or to tavernas.

The farming year

The next run of display cases deals with the farming year on Crete, showing and explaining the various tools that are used at every stage, from tilling the soil, to grinding wheat using watermills or hand querns. The exhibits include a vicious-looking plank set with sawblades and flints, resembling a medieval instrument of torture, but actually used for threshing grain. The operator stood or sat on the board while the animal pulled it round the threshing floor, the flint chips and saw blades breaking open the ears of wheat to

VORÍ

The area around Faistós, in southern Crete, is already well worth visiting for its major archaeological sites; now there is another incentive to come here, in the form of the excellent Museum of Cretan Ethnology in Vorí. The modern and sophisticated museum is housed in a building just to the south of the church.

release the grain. This, and the various ox-ploughs and sickles on display, are of a type that is quite likely to have been in use in the Mediterranean area from neolithic times until as recently as the 1970s and 1980s. Equally informative displays cover olive-oil production, viticulture and animal husbandry.

The enormous importance of sheep and goats to the Cretan economy is underlined by the displays on milk and cheese making, these two foods having provided the main source of protein in the Cretan diet for centuries. Meat was a rare luxury – sheep were kept principally for milk and wool, and cattle served primarily as draught animals; hens and pigeons supplied eggs, and rabbits and pigs were bred for meat. This diet was supplemented by hare, partridge and rabbit, trapped in the wild and once abundant on Crete.

Pottery and baskets

The ingenuity of Cretan potters is illustrated in the section on household vessels: jars for storing honey have a water trap around the rim to keep out ants and there are purpose-made vessels for storing pickled meat, salted fish, olives, oil, cereals, rusks, salt, water and wine – once the staples of the Cretan diet. Equally varied are the range of baskets used for harvesting and foraging, with marked regional variations in size and shape. Some baskets were used for storing grain, the inside having first been coated with cow-dung

plaster and whitewash to deter weevils and mice. Pungent herbs were also placed amongst the grain to prevent meal worm developing.

Weaving

The museum's most colourful displays cover the processes involved in converting raw wool into richly patterned cloth. Wonderful examples of bags, towels, aprons, blankets and saddle covers are displayed, the likes of which are very rarely seen for sale in Crete today. Modern weavers still use the Cretan hand loom, but their bright chemical dyes and leaping dolphin motifs are designed to please tourists – few now produce the traditional striped and geometric fabrics, in rich reds, greens and yellows obtained from vegetable dyes.

Vorí is 60km southwest of Iráklio, 3km north of Faistós. Museum of Cretan Ethnology open: daily 10am–6pm.

Bright weaves typical of the museum's exhibits

The tranquil atmosphere of Káto (Lower) Zákros

ZÁKROS

Zákros is actually two villages, separated by a winding road with spectacular eastward views to the sea. Áno (Upper) Zákros is a relatively modern and prosperous agricultural town with little to delay travellers except for a few shops and tavernas. Káto (Lower) Zákros is, by contrast, a tranquil fishing village which feels as if it were at the end of the earth, sitting on its own sheltered bay, with a good shingle beach, at the eastern tip of Crete. Yet, in its Minoan heyday, this was the site of a palace as important as that at Knosós.

History

The town surrounding the palace was partially excavated in 1901, but only as recently as 1962 was the palace itself discovered. The remains, which lie to the rear of the village, are being excavated with painstaking care because they have the potential to yield important information about life in Minoan times. Much of the site is waterlogged, because the sea level has risen – or rather, the island has tilted – since Minoan times, and there is the potential to find important organic remains. It also seems that the palace remains were placed under some kind of taboo following the disastrous fire that struck here, as at other palaces on Crete, in 1450BC. While parts of the Minoan town were reoccupied, nothing was touched in the palace, and archaeologists have even found intact bowls containing olives preserved as fresh as if they had just been picked, as well as numerous fine liturgical vessels and a considerable number of undeciphered Linear A clay tablets.

Trade with the East

Uniquely on Crete, this palace and town was built around a harbour, the remains of which now lie below sea level. Trade goods found by the excavators indicate that this was Minoan Crete's main gateway to the Orient, the point from which Minoan traders may have sailed to Egypt and beyond. Finds from the site include copper ingots identified as coming from Cyprus, gold and jewels from the Nile Delta and both elephant and rhinoceros ivory, possibly from Syria. In return, Cretans would have traded dyed wool, metal vases and silver-inlaid cups; we know this from tomb paintings (dated 1520–1420BC) in Upper Egypt depicting Minoan emissaries bearing just such goods as gifts, and described, in the accompanying hieroglyphs, as 'from the land of Keftiu', the name that the Egyptians gave to Crete.

Workshops

Minoan Zákros was also an important manufacturing centre and tools found on the site indicate that many of the rooms on the west side of the palace were used as foundries and workshops by pattern-makers, smiths, stone-workers and jewellers, potters and perfume-makers. Stores of unworked marble and steatite, a soft carvable rock like soapstone, were also found, and a marvellous jug (now in the Archaeological Museum in Iráklio (see page 32) carved from rock crystal.

The palace

This all suggests that the immediate environs of the palace were used by craftsmen working under the direct patronage or control of the palace inhabitants. As for the palace itself, it has a number of unusual features, including a unique circular chamber, fed by a spring, in the living quarters to the east of the court. This was surrounded by pillars to support a roof and has eight steps leading down into it. The chamber has been interpreted both as an aquarium and as a swimming pool – if so, it is the very first example of a prehistoric swimming pool ever identified. *Zákros is 170km east of Iráklio, 44km southeast of Sitiá. The Palace open: daily 9am–4pm. Free.*

The recently discovered Minoan palace

ZARÓS

The large village of Zarós is set high on the southern foothills of the Psilorítis range of mountains and is surrounded by a cluster of worthwhile churches and monasteries. The reason for Zarós being located where it is becomes apparent if you stop for a coffee in the village and explore the pretty side streets, with their colourful displays of pot plants. Water is very abundant here, running down the sides of the streets and splashing into stone troughs – numerous springs discharge from the hills behind the village, and in Roman times these were channelled into an artificial watercourse and carried to the town of Górtina, some 13km south.

Zarós is 54km southwest of Iráklio.
Churches open all day. Free.

water gushes from the mouths of wild creatures with flowing locks – possibly intended as lions. The fountain probably dates from the 15th century, while the monastery itself was founded a century earlier, and dedicated to St Antony, patron saint of hermits. The double-naved church is full of ancient icons, though the most famous, painted by the great Mikhaíl Damaskinós, are now in the Icon Museum in Iráklio (see page 38). The right-hand (southern) nave preserves darkened 14th-century frescos, depicting the Last Supper (in the apse) and scores of venerable saints and patriarchs, representing the Communion of the Saints, along the walls. Coming out of the church, do not miss the splendid views over the Mesarás Plain to be had from the terrace.

Venerable saints and patriarchs line the walls of Moní Vrondísion's ancient church (right)

Nearby:
Moní Vrondísion

To find Vrondísion monastery, continue through Zarós, turning right about 2km west of the village. The monastery entrance is shaded by two giant plane trees, and to the left is a small Venetian-era fountain featuring the now headless figures of Adam and Eve. Below them,

Visitors to Varsamónero's fresco-covered church will be enchanted by its rural setting

Varsamónero

To reach Varsamónero from Moní Vrondísion return to the main road and turn right, continuing to Voríza. Halfway up the hill in the middle of this village, look for a blue sign pointing left to Varsamónero. The bumpy concrete road gives way eventually to a dirt track, which leads for 2.5km to the church. This is set in a peaceful spot alone among the hills. The exterior is very simple – it has been cited as an example of Venetian influence on Byzantine architecture, but this runs to little more than a hint of Gothic dogtooth decoration and a carved Venetian coat of arms over the westernmost door.

This door, as becomes apparent when you step into the church, leads into a narthex, or antechamber to the main body of the double-naved church. The whole of the interior is covered in richly coloured frescos. The oldest are in the northern nave; dating to 1321, they depict the Life of the Virgin. Within the lovely iconostasis, (the wooden screen carved with vine-leaves that separates the church from the apse) there are scenes

from the Life of Christ, including his Baptism and Ascension, and his Entombment and Resurrection .

In the southern nave the frescos, painted in 1406–7, depict scenes from the Life of St John the Baptist. Right opposite the entrance door is the scene in which Salome dances to entertain Herod, while his guests are tucking into a sumptuous banquet. In the next scene to the left, John the Baptist is beheaded. On the pillar behind these two scenes, the elongated figure of the Baptist with long and straggly hair has been compared to the work of El Greco.

In the third part of the church, there is a little apse set into the southeastern wall. The frescos here, painted around 1431, depict Christ celebrating communion surrounded by a heavenly host of saints and angels. The remaining frescos depict the exploits of the soldier-saint Phanourios, to whom this church is dedicated. On the opposite wall there are several further scenes from the Life of Christ, and a scene in which demons are being spewed out of the mouth of a demented man.

BYZANTINE CHURCHES

In AD293 the Roman Empire, now so large that it covered almost all of modern Europe and the Near East, was split, for ease of administration, into eastern and western divisions. From AD330 the eastern empire began to grow in stature and independence when Constantine the Great founded the new city of Constantinopolis (modern Istanbul) on the site of a former Greek colony called Byzantium.

From Byzantium came the name for a new style of art and architecture that started here when the Church of the Apostles (now Ayía Sophia) was built in 537. Characterised by round arches, circles, domes and rich mosaic work (from which fresco later developed) this style became the norm for church architecture in the Eastern Empire and beyond, lasting right up to the present.

The churches of Crete

Crete has one surviving church from the early Byzantine period – the 6th-century Áyios Títos, at Górtina (see page 48). By contrast there are several hundred churches and monasteries from the 10th to 17th centuries, surviving in various states of repair. Some of the finest and most important have been restored, but most remain untouched, their frescos cracked and blackened by centuries of candle soot, their simple walls leaning this way and that.

Most are simple churches with a nave, dome and apse. Separating the nave from the apse is an iconostasis, a carved and often gilded wooden screen on which icons (see page 38) are displayed. The iconostasis serves to screen the altar since, in the Orthodox liturgy, key moments, such as the mystic transformation of bread and wine into Christ's flesh and blood, are performed in secret, away from the eyes of the congregation. Larger churches may have a second or even a third nave, each with its own iconostasis and apse, and occasionally a narthex, an entrance vestibule running the width of the church at the western end.

Today's churches (left) continue the style of their predecessors at Samonás (above), Kanousi (right) and Episkopí (far right)

Frescos

Frescos are closely related to the architecture of the church. The dome, which represents the heavens, is usually painted with the figure of Christ Pantocrator (Ruler of All) looking down on the congregation, his hands raised in blessing and to display the wounds of his Crucifixion. In smaller churches without domes, Christ Pantocrator appears in the apse instead. In larger churches, the apse may feature the Last Supper, with Christ in the centre, or more probably the Communion of the Saints, with Christ as the officiating priest surrounded by angels, saints and patriarchs.

Many frescos are also dated by an inscription, often located in the apse, or at the rear of the church, on the west wall. Occasionally there will also be a portrait of the donor and his family – look for this by the west door, or at the western end of the north wall of the nave.

Iráklio

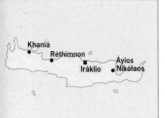

Despite its dusty streets and concrete buildings, Iráklio remains a Cretan city at heart, with plenty of street life to make up for the uninspiring architecture (for map of route see page 28/29). *Allow 1½ hours.*

Start at the Archaeological Museum and walk around the western curve of **Platía Eleftherías (1)** past the up-market Astoria Capsis Hotel and several shops selling reproductions of Minoan pottery and jewellery. A few Irákliots still come to take coffee in the square, once the city's social heart, but huge tour buses calling at the museum have destroyed the former tranquillity. Turn right down Odós Daidálos to indulge in a spot of window shopping. Smart boutiques and jewellery shops line both sides of the pedestrianised street.

This leads down to **Platía Venizélou (2)**, the city's other main square, lined with cafés, pastry shops and newspaper kiosks. The square is almost one large outdoor café and is liveliest at night. In the centre is the Morosini Fountain, built in 1628 by order of the city's Venetian governor, Francesco Morosini. The lower basin is carved with seahorses and cherubs, while the upper bowl rests on four lions, the lion being the symbol of St Mark and Venice.

Turn left here and cross the next road to find the city's bustling market in Odós 1866. This narrow street is lined with shops selling herbs, nuts, honey, embroidery, rugs, shoes, cheese, sponges and much more.

The fish market is at the very top of the street, where the aroma of coffee wafts from numerous cafés.

Odós 1866, the market street, leads to this pretty kiosk

From Iráklio's Venetian fortress there are good views of the harbourside Arsenal and the city beyond

One of these is set around a pretty kiosk converted from an old Turkish fountain, while behind is the Bembo Fountain of 1588 featuring a headless Roman statue from Ierápetra.

A walk through the fish market (in Odós Kartérou) introduces you to the many varieties of fish found in local waters. The street leads to the peaceful **Platía Ayía Aikateríni (3)** with its three churches. The biggest is the ornate 19th-century cathedral. More interesting is its small 16th-century predecessor, alongside, containing an intricately carved iconostasis (1759) and charming scenes depicting Adam and Eve. On the opposite side of the square, the church of St Catherine of Sinai (Ayía Aikateríni) houses the Icon Collection (see page 38). Follow the alley behind the church until it meets Odós 1821, then turn left back

to Platía Venizélou. Continue through the square, noting the Municipal Gallery on the right, housed in the church of Áyios Márcos, fronted by a 15th-century Renaissance arcade.

Almost next door is the Venetian armoury, now the City Hall, fronted by a Venetian loggia (arcade) of 1626 decorated with military emblems. Behind is the church of Áyios Títos, rebuilt in 1856 and housing the precious skull of the saint who was the friend of St Paul and first bishop of Crete (see page 48). The skull is not on display but is occasionally brought out to be shown to the faithful.

Odós 25 Augoústou leads downhill from here to the harbour, and its imposing Venetian fortress (see page 28); the walk to the fortress and out along the sea wall is well worth doing for the views.

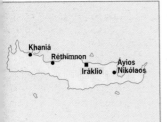

The Lasíthiou Plateau

The famous windmills of the Lasíthiou plateau are highly photogenic, but increasingly rare to find. Even so, the plateau scenery is rewarding in its own right and certainly justifies a visit. *Allow at least 4 hours – all day if you plan to visit the Dhíktaen Cave (Dhiktaio Andro).*

From Iráklio head east on the National Highway (heading for Áyios Nikólaos). After 25km look for the right turn, clearly signposted to Kastélli/Tzermiadho/Lasíthiou Plateau. This road follows the broad and scenic valley of the Aposelémis river to Potamiés.

After this village the hills enclosing the Lasíthiou plateau loom ahead like a cliff wall. Note the knob on the crest of the ridge, known as 'The Nail'. This outcrop was the site of a Minoan peak sanctuary where, intriguingly, the old religious rites continued to be practised for some 400 years after the final destruction of the Minoan palace culture in 1450BC.

Progress is slower after the village of Goniés as the road begins to twist and turn. At the next junction turn right and continue upwards. Far below you will see the fertile Mokhós Plain. After 3km you will come to a side-turning (left) to Krási, worth a detour for coffee and to admire the massive plane tree on the main square while watching coach-borne tourists link arms to see how many people it takes to encircle the trunk. Another detour lies 2km to the right: Moní Kerá (Kerá

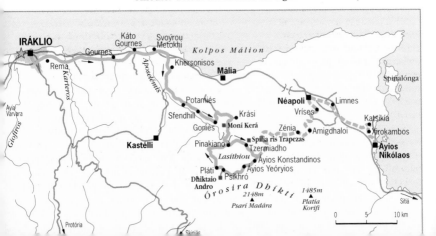

Tourist trap: rugs and embroidery for sale in Tzermiadho, Lasíthiou's main town

Monastery) is largely modern but its hillside site guarantees sweeping views north to Dhía Island over the Gulf of Iráklio (Kolpos Iráklio).

Shortly afterwards you will reach the Selí Ambélou pass (900m), where you can admire southward views that take in the whole Lasíthiou plateau. Rows of ruined windmills line the crest of the ridge to the east of the pass. Descending into the plain, the view ahead is of Psarí Madára, at 2,148m the highest peak in the Dhíktaen mountain range.

At the next junction you will encounter scenes of extensively cultivated ground interspersed with fruit orchards. Rusting iron windmills are everywhere, but they look far from romantic unless you are here in summer when their canvas sails are unfurled to catch the wind (see also page 62).

Turn left to begin a circular tour of the plateau villages. Tzermiadho is the principal town, full of old balconied houses hung with brightly coloured rugs and embroidery for sale. On the far side of the village, a signpost points to the Trapéza Cave (also called Krónio Cave), site of recent excavations, and easily reached by a short footpath.

In Áyios Konstandinos it is well worth stopping to visit the clearly signposted Cretan Folk Museum set in a typical Cretan village house built in 1800. Psikhró is a scruffy, commercialised village catering to the many visitors to the Dhíktaen Cave (see page 70). From here the road continues round the plateau rim back to Pinakiano for the return journey to Iráklio.

Alternatively, you can continue your tour by backtracking through Áyios Konstandinos and taking the right turning beyond the village for Neápoli and Áyios Nikólaos.

Moní Kerá – open: daily
8am–1pm and 3–7pm.
Cretan Folk Museum – open:
daily 10am–6pm.

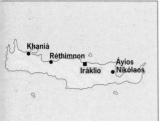

Cretan Archaeology

This route takes in some of Crete's star archaeological attractions – the Roman capital of Górtina and the Minoan palaces of Faistós and Ayía Triádha, ending up in the peaceful resort of Mátala. *Allow all day for the tour (with an early start) and consider spending the night in Mátala, then driving on to Ayía Galíni to take the Amári Valley tour (page 136) in the reverse direction to Réthimnon.*

Take the westward road out of Iráklio, following signs to Réthimnon. Where you meet the Old Road/New Road junction,

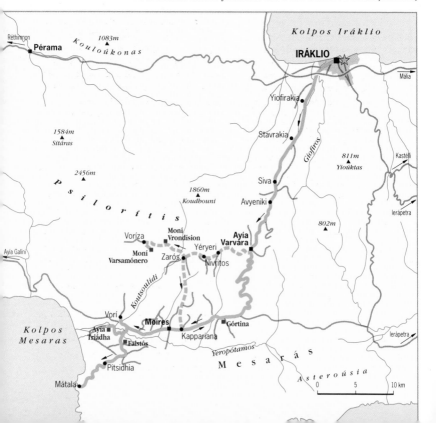

Faistós is a feast for visitors in search of Crete's ancient past

5km out of town, turn left following the New Road signs but pass under the highway rather than joining the sliproad. From here on it is easy driving all the way to Górtina, but if you are planning to make this a two-day trip, you can make a two-hour diversion in Ayía Varvára to visit Zarós and its churches.

Turn right in Ayía Varvára to reach Zarós, a pleasant flower-filled village. Continue through the village and turn right, after 2km, up a road signposted to the Moní Vrondísion (see page 80) worth visiting for its frescos and views over the fertile Mesarás plain. Returning to the main road, turn right and continue to Voríza. Halfway up the hill in the middle of the village a blue sign points left to the Moní Varsamónero. Drive slowly down the bumpy concrete road which soon gives way to a dirt track. This simple church (see page 81) enjoys a lovely peaceful setting.

Return to Zarós and, just before leaving the village, take the right turn signposted Moíres. This fast new road leads to Kappariana. Turn left for Górtina (see page 48), the ancient Roman capital of Crete. It is tempting to explore for hours – though you should bear in mind that Ayía Triádha shuts at 3pm (2.30pm on Sunday) and Faistós at 7pm (6pm in the low season; 3pm on Sunday) and plan your day accordingly.

Drive west (signposted Vorí) for 14km then take the left turn clearly signposted to Faistós. You cannot miss the site (see page 44), but Ayía Triádha is not so easily found: from the Faistós car park head south towards Mátala, but turn right immediately beyond the end of the car park (opposite the little church that stands within the fenced area on the left). The 3km track winds through countryside scarred by a forest fire and ends abruptly, with Ayía Triádha nowhere in sight. In fact the palace lies in pine trees below you and to the left (see page 46).

Return to Faistós and either turn right to descend to Mátala, or consider one last diversion, to see the outstanding Museum of Cretan Ethnology at Vorí, which stays open until 6pm daily. To get there, drive back to the main valley road, turn left and first right into Vorí, where the museum is in the village centre behind the church (see page 76).

Mátala (see page 66) makes a relaxing end to the day's excursion. If you are staying the night, aim to settle down into a west-facing café by sunset to watch the sun go down in a blaze of colour.

Western Crete

Western Crete consists of the two provinces (*nomoi*) of Réthimnon and Khaniá, with populations of 69,290 and 133,060 respectively (23,595 and 65,519 in the provincial capitals). Both provinces are dominated by high mountains which rise gently from the northern coast, where most of the towns and villages are located, dropping very steeply to the narrow coastal strip on the southern side of the island.

Beaches

Beach lovers looking for the choicest spots in Western Crete should consider the strip from Khaniá to Málame, the lonely beaches stretching south from Falasárna and the idyllic coral islands of Elafonísi.

Mountain peaks

In Khaniá, the peaks of the Levká Óra (the White Mountains) fill the horizon whenever you turn your eyes to the south. They are named after the snows that cover the long east–west ridge for six months of the year (November to April) and because the grey-white limestone screes that rise above the tree-line look like snow during the summer months. This is serious mountaineering country and those who make it to the top of Pákhnes (2,453m) have been building a massive cairn on the summit for some years. Their objective is to erode the 3m height difference between this, Crete's second highest peak, and Tímios Stavrós (2,456m), the island's highest peak, also referred to as Mount Psilorítis or Mount Idha, located at the western end of the Psilorítis range in the adjacent province of Réthimnon. Climbing Tímios Stavrós does not represent quite the same challenge since well-marked shepherds' tracks lead up to the chapel on the summit. Roads also penetrate a long way up the northern slope of the range to the

Ídhaean Cave, where Zeus spent his childhood, suckled by wild goats, and where Crete's first ski centre has been established.

Natural beauty

If eastern Crete has the lion's share of the island's archaeology, western Crete wins on natural beauty. The region has numerous deep, water-eroded ravines – not just the overcrowded and popular Samaria Gorge, but also the Thériso, Ímbros and Kurtalióti ravines (see pages 132,138 and 140), the almost undiscovered 7km-long Ayía Iríni Gorge (starting 20km north of Soúyia) and the Arádena Gorge to the west of Khóra Sfakíon. This is also the richest part of the island for botanists, with far less soil under cultivation and a great range of habitats, from beaches and cliffs to swamps and river estuaries, where wading birds and terrapins add to the biological diversity.

Provincial capitals

Above all, western Crete has the island's two most attractive towns, in Khaniá and Réthimnon, the provincial capitals. Both have colourful harbours guarded by fine Venetian fortresses and are lined with cafés and tavernas. Réthimnon perhaps preserves more of its Turkish heritage, with delicate minarets of golden sandstone soaring above the domed Venetian churches, and beautifully carved wooden balconies, typical of Ottoman-style architecture, projecting from upper storeys. Khaniá, by contrast, is more of a Venetian city, its narrow streets lined with classical palazzi decorated with wrought-iron balconies. Here and there, a narrow gate provides a view of delightful patio gardens or shady, flower-filled courtyards, and, also like Venice, sleek cats prowl the streets as if they were the true owners.

Orange groves
Travelling west, the national highway runs out soon after Khaniá, giving way to narrow country roads (though the western highway extension is under construction) that weave in and out of huge citrus groves. During spring the scent of orange blossom is overpowering – the air is thick with the sweet smell, and equally sweet fruit that is ready for picking from late October. Green-skinned, even when ripe, Crete's oranges really are ambrosial and one taste will make you realise why they are in such demand in the far-off markets of Athens. Away from this intensively cultivated part of the coastal plain there are some of the loneliest spots on Crete, and some of the least-visited and most unspoiled villages on the whole island.

Less-developed Western Crete is full of flowers

WESTERN CRETE

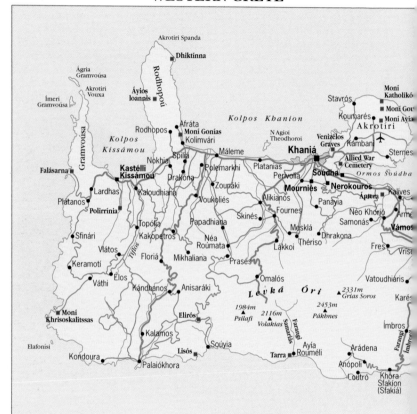

Akrotíri Spanda
Dhiktínna
Rodhopoú
Ágria Gramvoúsa
Akrotíri Vouxa
Áyios Ioannis
Ímeri Gramvoúsa
Afráta
Rodhopos
Moni Gonías
Kolimvári
Kolpos Kissámou
Nokhiá
Spiliá
Máleme
Kolpos Khaníon
N Agioi Theodhoroi
Stavrós
Moní Katholikó
Moní Gou
Moní Ayía
Koumarés
Akrotíri
Venizélos Graves
Kámban
Khaniá
Sternes
Falásarna
Gramvoúsa
Kastélli Kissámou
Polemarkhi
Platanias
Allied War Cemetery
Ormos Soúdha
Drakóna
Zouráki
Perivólia
Soúdha
Plátanos
Lardhas
Kaloudhianá
Voukoliés
Alikianós
Mourniés
Nerokouros
Áptera
Kalíves
Polirrínia
Panávia
Néo Khorió
Arme
Sfinári
Topólia
Papadhiana
Skinés
Fournes
Mesklá
Samonás
Vámos
Kakópetros
Néa Roúmata
Dhrakona
Thériso
Fres
Vriste
Vlátos
Floriá
Mikhaliana
Prasés
Lákkoi
Keramotí
Éros
Anisaráki
Omalós
Vatoudhiáris
Váthi
Kándhanos
Levká Óri
2331m Grías Soros
Karés
Moní Khrisoskalítssas
Elirós
1984m Psilafi
2116m Volakias
Samariás
Farangi
2453m Pákhnes
Ímbros
Farangi
Elafonísi
Kalamos
Lisós
Soúyia
Tarra
Ayía Rouméli
Arádena
Anópoli
Khóra Sfakion (Sfakiá)
Kondoura
Palaiókhora
Loutró

0   10   20 km

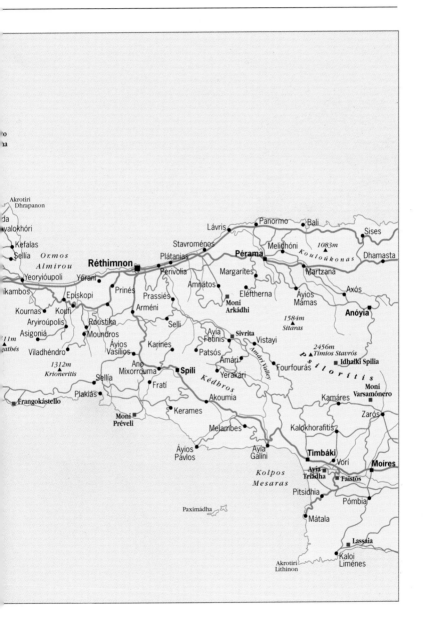

Khaniá

*K*haniá easily wins the title of most beautiful harbour in Crete, lined as it is with pastel-painted houses with orange-tiled roofs, varied by the strikingly exotic domes of the Mosque of the Janissaries. Enclosing the whole harbour is the 16th-century sea wall, built of cream-coloured stone, leaving open only a narrow entrance channel through which boats slip under the watchful eye of the Firkás tower (now housing the Naval Museum – see page 97).

Despite such defences, Khaniá fell to the Turks in 1645, the year in which the Mosque of the Janissaries was built. The Turks made Khaniá the capital of Crete, and so it remained until 1971 when the title passed to Iráklio.

The legacy of Venetian rule is visible everywhere in the city, from the beautiful town houses of the old city (see Walk on page 128) to the massive Arsenal, or shipyard, lining the eastern waterfront. The Turks built their city, known as Kastélli, on the hill above the mosque. The massive walls of their fortifications are visible from the waterfront, but bombing in the last war destroyed most of the old houses. Recent excavations at the heart of Kastélli (left open and visible on the left-hand side of Odós Karneváro) have revealed the tantalising remains of a massive Minoan town, whose name (preserved in Linear B clay tablets) was Kydonia.

Archaeological Museum

Khaniá's Archaeological Museum is housed in a large but simple 13th-century church built to serve the city's long-demolished Franciscan friary, established under Venetian rule. The exhibits provide an overview of the type of material typically found on Minoan sites in Khaniá province. There are few outstanding works of art, though cases in the north aisle contain interesting fertility figures, and there is a toy dog made from clay that was found in a child's grave.

At the eastern end of the church are

several statues and mosaics of Roman date, including an appealing marble figure of Aphrodite and some highly accomplished 3rd-century mosaics from a townhouse in Khaniá. One contains depictions of the seasons and another shows Dionysos discovering Ariadne on the island of Naxos (see page 34), while

a third, depicting the myth of Poseidon and Amymone, is enlivened by a little vignette of fighting cockerels at the top. Off the south aisle is a little garden littered with ancient masonry whose centrepiece is a 10-sided fountain dating from the Turkish occupation.

Odós Khalídon 21. Open: Tuesday to Sunday, 8.30am–3pm. Closed: Monday. Admission charge.

Historical Museum

The little-visited Historical Museum is located in an elegant but faded townhouse in the city's turn-of-the-century southern suburbs. This area became fashionable from 1898 when Crete gained limited autonomy from Turkish rule, and when Prince George of Greece, appointed High Commissioner (in effect ruler of the island) chose this part of the city for his official residence. The relevance of all this becomes clear once you enter the museum, which is virtually a shrine to the heroes of the Cretan resistance and the political figures who brought about freedom from Turkish rule, and unification with Greece. Elifthérios Venizélos, for example (see page 98) gets a whole room to himself, to the right of the entrance, and the downstairs corridor bristles with displays of the beautifully decorated swords and guns of Cretan freedom fighters.

At the foot of the staircase at the end of the corridor is the museum's star exhibit, a rare 16th-century cupboard carved in relief with hunting scenes. The

Khaniá's domed Mosque of the Janissaries adds an oriental touch to the harbour scene

KHANIÁ TOWN PLAN

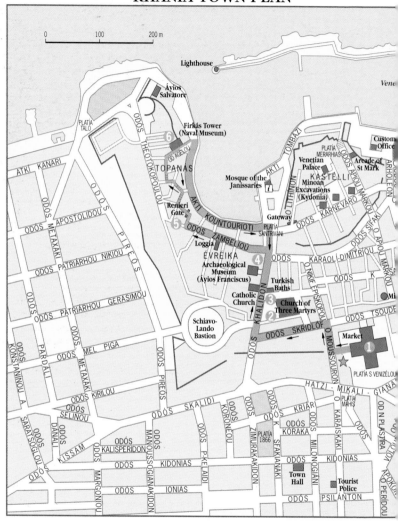

0   100   200 m

Lighthouse

Áyios Salvatore

PLATIA TALO

Firkás Tower (Naval Museum)

Custom Office

PLATIA MERARHIAS

Venetian Palace

Arcade of St Mark

ODÓS THEOTOKOPOULOU

OD AGELOU

TOPANÁS

KASTÉLLI

Mosque of the Janissaries

Minoan Excavations (Kydonia)

AKTÍ KOUNTOURIÓTI

AKTÍ LITHINON

AKTÍ TOMBÁZI

ODÓS APIOU MARKOU

ODÓS ARHOLEON

ATKÍ KANÁRI

ODÓS PIREOS

Renieri Gate

Gateway

KARNEVÁRO

ODÓS APOSTOLIDOU

ODÓS METAXAKI

ODÓS ZAMBELIOU

PLATIA SANTRIVANI

ODÓS

ODÓS SIFAKI

ODÓS APIOU MARKOU

Loggia

ÉVRÉIKA

ODÓS

KARAOLÍ-DIMITRÍOU

ODÓS PATRIARHOU NIKIOU

Archaeological Museum (Áyios Franciscus)

ODÓS NIKIF EPISKOPOU

KONDILAKI

ODÓS

K

ODÓS

KHALIDON

Turkish Baths

Catholic Church

Church of Three Martyrs

Mi

ODÓS PATRIARHOU GERASIMOU

ODÓS TSOUDE

PARDALI

KONSTANTINOU A

ODÓS METAXAKI

MEL PIGA

Schiavo-Lando Bastion

ODÓS SKRIDLÓF

Market

PIREOS

ODÓS

O MOUSSOUROU

PLATIA S VENIZÉLOU

HATZÍ - MIKÁLI - GIANA

ODÓS KIRILOU

SARATSOGLOU

DANALI

ODÓS SELINOU

KISSAM

ODÓS SKALIDI

ODÓS KORONEOU

ODÓS ZIMURAKAKIDON

KRIÁRI

O PLATIA MAHIS

ODÓS KARAISKAKI

OD N PLIASTRA

MARGONIOU

ODÓS KALISPERIDON

ODÓS MANOUSSOGIANNAKIDON

ODÓS P.KELAIDI

KIDONIAS

PLATIA 1866

KORAKA

STEFANAKI

ODÓS

MILONOGIANI

KIDONIAS

APOKOR

 O PERIDOU

ODÓS

IONIAS

Town Hall

Tourist Police

ODÓS IPSILANTON

---

stairs themselves feature grim reminders of World War II – a Nazi flag, an execution stake ominously hacked about at head height and horrifying photographs of Cretan peasants and English soldiers bludgeoning German parachutists to death. Two rooms full of antique textiles and a magnificent nuptial

Maritime Crete at the Naval Museum

Naval Museum

Housed in Khaniá's Firkás tower, this museum explains far more than the naval history of Crete, though models of ships, from ancient Greek times until the present era, do figure large among the displays. Of more general interest is the splendid scale model of Khaniá in the 17th century, complete with its monasteries, synagogue, arsenal (dockyard) and fortifications. Alongside, a beautifully drawn map shows which of these Venetian structures have survived to this day – a surprisingly large number in fact.

For many visitors the upstairs displays on the Battle of Crete (see page 110) will probably prove the most enthralling. The story of the battle is told in detail through contemporary photographs, newspaper reports and war relics such as as a wedding dress made from parachute silk.
Aktí Kountourioti. Open: Tuesday to Sunday, 10am–4pm.Closed: Monday, Admission charge.

bed are often closed but are well worth seeing when possible.
Odós Sfakianáki 20. Open Monday to Friday 9am–1pm. Free.

Despite the presence of the airport and naval base, the Akrotíri peninsula has its peaceful spots

AKROTÍRI PENINSULA

The Akrotíri peninsula juts out like a clenched fist to the northeast of Khaniá, enclosing to the south the beautiful sweep of Soúdha Bay, much of which is out of bounds to ordinary mortals, being the site of a large NATO naval base. The once-peaceful peninsula is now the site of Crete's second airport, and this has stimulated major development as factories and distribution warehouses are constructed to take advantage of the airport's proximity. Even so, there are some wild and unspoiled areas to the north, including Stavrós, a pretty fishing village enclosed by high cliffs, where the final scenes in *Zorba the Greek* were filmed.

The Venizélos Graves

If you drive east out of Khaniá, following the signs for the airport, you will climb for some 4km until a sign on the left points to the Venizélos Graves. Here the Cretan hero and statesman, Elifthérios Venizélos, is buried, with his son, Sophoklés, on a beautiful and restful hilltop site high above Khaniá. If for no other reason, the panoramic views make this spot worth seeking out – additional attractions include a pleasant tree-shaded park (good for a lunchtime picnic) and the little Byzantine church of Profitis Ilías that stands close to the graves.

It was on this hill, in 1897, at a very tense moment in the Cretan War of Independence, that Cretan fighters raised the Greek flag in defiance of the Turks. The flag was almost instantly demolished by shells fired from a battleship in the harbour below, one of which also hit the church. The ship that fired the shells was itself sunk the next day, an act of divine revenge, according to devout Cretans.

Among the partisans who raised the Greek flag on that day was Elifthérios Venizélos (1864–1936), a prominent figure in the War of Independence , who went on to become prime minister of Greece in 1910. He survived one assassination attempt and, in 1935, having led an abortive republican coup was condemned to death by victorious monarchists. He avoided execution by fleeing to Paris where he died shortly after. To Cretans he remains a hero and an almost saintly figure.

Ayía Triádha

This 17th-century monastery lies 2km north of the airport. The sleepy monastic buildings show clearly the influence of Venetian architecture in, for example, the belltower that rises high above the entrance gate, and in the classical purity of the church façade. The church contains carved wooden choir stalls and there is a small display of vestments, icons and illuminated prayer books. _Closed from 2–5pm._

Gouvernéto and Katholikó

Keen walkers, and drivers prepared to take it slowly, can follow the track from the monastery that leads, after 4km, to the more remote Gouvernéto monastery. This dates from the 11th century, but is essentially a 16th-century complex, restored in 1821, with many fine Venetian-inspired details. Older still are the ruins of Katholikó, 25 minutes walk away on a well-defined path and beautifully sited in a ravine. This was founded early in the 11th century by St John the Hermit. Hundreds of pilgrims come here for his feast day, on 7 October, one of western Crete's most important religious festivals.

Ayía Triádha monastery (above) and moving memorials (left) to the victims of war

Soúdha Bay Allied War Cemetery

Another worthwhile stop is the Soúdha Bay Allied War Cemetery on the neck of land just north of Soúdha itself. Eucalyptus trees surround this peaceful and reflective spot on three sides, leaving open the fine views to Soúdha Bay, a lovely stretch of blue water framed by peaks and dotted with the aircraft carriers of the modern NATO fleet. Here are buried some 1,527 of the 2,000 Commonwealth soldiers who died in the Cretan campaign, many of them are anonymous and marked by a slab that simply says 'Known unto God'.

The Akrotíri peninsula lies immediately to the northeast of Khaniá.

Textiles in Anóyia (left), bust of El Greco in Fódhele (below) and theÍdhaean Cave (right) where Zeus may have spent his infancy

Nearby:

The Ídhaean Cave (Idhaiki Spilia)

South of Anóyia, a steep and winding road heads south into the mountains to Crete's only ski centre, and on to the Ídhaean Cave. Some claim that this cave was the true birthplace of Zeus (see page 34), rather than the Dhíktean Cave (see page 70) which lies further to the east. Others say that Zeus was born in the Dhíktean Cave but brought up in this cave. Certainly the cave has long been revered and is mentioned in the writings of both Plato and Pythagoras. Archaeologists are working to find out more, and the cave is closed to the public as a result.

If you venture up here in summer, when excavation work is in progress, you can watch the painstaking work of sifting the cave deposits. Another reason for coming here would be for the wildflowers: at this high altitude (1,500m and above), spring comes up to eight weeks later than on the coast, so you can see a mass of bulbs and other wildflowers as late as June. The high pastures also support seasonal grazing, and the shepherds still use the traditional circular stone huts that dot the landscape as places of shelter, and as dairies, where the animals are milked and the milk made into cheese.

ANÓYIA

Anóyia is well placed to serve as a base for exploring the villages and sights that lie along the northern flank of the Psilorítis mountain range. Part of Anóyia's appeal lies in its reputation as a weaving centre; tour buses bring people here to watch weavers at work and to shop for blankets, wall hangings and shoulder bags of brightly coloured woven wool. The town has a traditional air, but most of the buildings date from the post-war era: Anóyia was destroyed in August 1944 for being, in the words of the German commander on Crete 'a centre of British espionage and an asylum for resistance bands'. *Anóyia is 35km southwest of Iráklio.*

Fódhele

Fódhele is promoted as the birthplace of the artist, El Greco (born Doménikos Theotokópoulos). In fact it is more likely that he was born in Iráklio, but

ΔΟΜΕΝΙΚΟΣ ΘΕΟΤΟΚΟΠΟΥΛΟΣ
EL GRECO

this does not stop the village exploiting the El Greco association, even to the extent that his family's house has been identified and restored to pristine newness. The house is signposted from the village and delightfully located in an orange grove about 1km from the village centre. Opposite the house is the lovely domed church of the Panayía (the Virgin), built in the early 14th century but incorporating the nave of its 8th-century predecessor. The frescos (dated 1323) are far from complete but have been well restored and depict saints, angels and scenes from the Life of Christ.

Fódhele is 27km west of Iráklio.

Tílisos

From Fódhele, a new road leads north to join the Old Highway, now superseded by the New Highway running along the north coast. From here the best way to Anóyia is via Tílisos, a town which, remarkably, preserves something like its ancient Minoan name – it is called Turiso in Linear B clay tablets. It is also the site of three large Minoan villas dating from the New Palace period (1700–1450BC). These have survived remarkably intact – in the case of Villa C, the walls stand almost to first-floor level, with flights of stone stairs leading up to what would have been the living quarters. The villas have features similar to the great palace sites, such as lustral basins (for washing and anointing visitors), shrines, treasuries and rooms full of giant storage jars. Unusually, there are also rooms in Villas A and C with drains leading through the outer walls: these have been interpreted as possible toilets.

Tílisos is midway between Iráklio and Anóyia. Tílisos villas open: daily 8.30am–3pm. Admission charge.

The harbour at Kastélli, with views to the Rodhopós peninsula

KASTÉLLI

Kastélli (sometimes known as Kastélli Kissámou) is a bustling and prosperous town serving the local agricultural community. Here you are likely to come across furniture makers at work outside their workshops, cobblers making Cretan riding boots and old-fashioned bakers using wood-fired ovens. The museum in the main square has long been closed for restoration. If it ever re-opens it is worth visiting for its fine collection of Roman statuary, including finds from Dhiktínna, the 2nd-century AD temple that sits at the tip of the Rodhopós peninsula, to the east of Kastélli. A rough track leads across the peninsula to the temple site but it is not recommended for cars. Instead, it is better to hire a boat from nearby Kolimvári (see page 106).
Kastélli is 43km west of Khaniá.

Nearby:
Polirrínia

Some 7km south of Kastélli is the ancient city of Polirrínia, a rare example of the kind of city that developed in the post-Minoan era. Cretan society ceased to be highly centralised, and scores, if not hundreds, of small communities were set up, each controlling their own territory. It was probably the lack of water that resulted in Polirrínia's abandonment, though the inhabitants did not move far – only down to the base of the hill to the site of today's village, where springs are abundant. From this village, several paths lead uphill to the church (usually locked) built on the site of a Hellenistic-era temple and incorporating Roman masonry into its external walls. From the church, a broad path leads through flower-filled olive groves to the massive walls that surrounded the ancient city. Higher still are the jumbled ruins of fortifications built when the site was briefly re-occupied in the 10th to 13th centuries. Winding through the walls are goat tracks that eventually lead to the crest of the hill, from where there are fine views over the Gulf of Kíssamos (Kolpos Kissámou).

Falásarna

The ancient port city of Falásarna lies to the west of Kastélli, and is well worth visiting both for its ruins and for the huge and little-visited sandy beach. Approaching Falásarna from Plátanos, there are fine views down onto the beach and across the Gramvoúsa peninsula. The port ruins are some 1.5km from the Falásarna Hotel, near the end of a rough track. Passing masses of polythene tunnels, you know you have nearly reached the site when you pass a large and prominent stone 'throne' on the left (its real purpose is not known). The site is littered with equally huge blocks of tufa, tumbled from the ancient city's collapsed walls.

The entrance is located next to a prominent circular tower, also part of the city's 3rd-century BC defences, alongside of which is a square cistern with its original plaster-and-pitch lining intact. From here you descend to the flat harbour basin, once under water, but now left high and dry by tectonic movements that have lifted this western end of Crete by about 9m. Square trenches in the base of the harbour have been left open by archaeologists, at the bottom of which you can see massive masonry blocks jumbled up with pebbles. The theory is that the harbour, built in the 4th century

BC, had virtually fallen out of use by the 1st century, but, being enclosed and hidden, was used by pirates as a base for attacking Roman ships. Once the Romans had conquered Crete they therefore, deliberately and permanently, blocked the harbour entrance with these huge stones.

If you have the energy, you can climb the hill to the northwest of the harbour, passing little Áyios Yeóryios church, to reach the hilltop *acropolis*, with its fine views. Alternatively, you can simply enjoy swimming from the nearby beach and exploring the many rock pools.

You can enjoy the beach to yourself at little-visited Falásarna

KHÓRA SFAKÍON

Khóra Sfakíon is a pretty and unspoiled fishing village on the south coast which makes the ideal base for a hideaway holiday if all you want to do is walk, swim and enjoy good food in waterside tavernas. It is also a stopping point for ferries operating along the south coast; services operate daily out of Khóra Sfakíon, calling at Ayá Rouméli (for the Samaria Gorge – see page 124) and at Soúyia, Palaiókhora and Gávdhos island (for all of which see pages 118–19). The timetable changes regularly, so be sure to check when and where the ferry boat actually calls! The larger boats cannot get into Khóra Sfakíon's harbour, and so dock just outside the town.

West of Khóra Sfakíon

Only one road goes west of Khóra Sfakíon, a twisting, steep and narrow road that drops vertiginously away to the south and is not recommended to

nervous drivers. This passes, just to the west of the town, a group of beachside caves. One of these is named the Cave of Daskaloyiánnis in honour of the 18th-century rebel who led the Cretan struggle against Turkish rule and reputedly used the cave as a hideout. Daskaloyiánnis came from Anópoli, the next village along the road, once a rebel stronghold, now renowned for its carpets of spring wildflowers. Here there is a choice of routes: on foot to Loutró, or by car, along a newly made road, to Arádena. Loutró, about two hours walk due south along a steep downhill footpath, is the site of an ancient harbour, to which St Paul was heading when his boat was blown off course. (He was eventually shipwrecked off Malta.) It sits on a very beautiful bay, with the added attraction that the only way in and out is by boat or

Once a sleepy fishing village, Khóra Sfakíon now has a choice of hotels

on foot – though this has not deterred recent villa development.

Arádena, by contrast, is a near-deserted village and a delight to explore. It sits on a stony arid plateau, backed by the Levká Óri (White Mountains) whose peaks rise sheer behind. Like several other isolated and abandoned villages on Crete, the former inhabitants migrated to other parts of the island – or even overseas – in order to make a better living. Some have returned and are starting to restore the decayed buildings, and one wealthy family has donated the new iron bridge that provides access to the village across the spectacular Arádena Gorge. Hand-painted signs in the village point down deserted cobbled streets to the white-domed church of Mikhaíl Arkhángelos, with its 14th-century frescos, just visible through the door-grille if the church is locked. To the right of the church is the old road, a broad pebbled path that was the only way into and out of the village until the new bridge was built. The path leads to the edge of the ravine and then plunges down into it, following a zig-zag path up the other side. If you follow this path (well worth doing for views and the wildflowers) allow about an hour to reach the top on the other side.

Wild flowers abound in and around the spectacular Arádena Gorge

East of Khóra Sfakíon

East of Khóra Sfakíon the countryside is flat and intensively cultivated, with a rash of villa developments. The only historic site of note is the atmospheric Frangokástello, a Venetian fortress that looks remarkably complete from a distance, though only the external walls survive to any height. The castle was built in 1371 ostensibly to protect the southern coast against piratical raids. In fact the castle was more often used for quelling the local population. Nearly 400 men lost their lives in this peaceful spot in 1828 when Cretan insurrectionists, led by Khátzi Mikhális Daliánis, were massacred by an overwhelming force of Turkish soldiers. Local people say that a ghostly army, known as the *drossoulítes* (literally 'dew shades') returns at dawn to dance on the plain in front of the castle on the anniversary of the massacre, 17 May. Despite a grim history, the castle is tailor-made for children to explore and stands beside a fine and sandy beach, washed by warm and shallow waters.

Khóra Sfakíon is 75km southeast of Khaniá.

KOLIMVÁRI

Much of the coastline west of Khaniá has been developed for tourism and only when you get as far as Kolimvári do you return to the real Crete. Local people come here for the renowned seafood restaurants, but few tourists follow in their wake. Those who do will find an attractive and self-confident town with a pebble beach, numerous rock pools and crystal-clear waters teeming with small fish.

Kolimvári has escaped development

The Dhiktínna

Boat operators offer trips from Kolimvári out to the northeastern tip of the Rodhopós peninsula, site of the Dhiktínna, one of the ancient world's most famous temples. The Dhiktínna or Diktiynnaion thrived from Hellenistic times (the 3rd century BC) through to the Roman era. The goddess Díktynna was, like Diana, a huntress, usually depicted with her dogs, protectress of the mountains and countryside. She was worshipped all over the Greek, and subsequently the Roman world, with temples to her honour in Marseilles, Athens and Sparta. This was her chief sanctuary and it has been suggested that Díktynna represents the survival of a deity from Minoan times – she may have derived from the mountain mother goddess worshipped in Minoan peak sanctuaries. This temple was visible from far out at sea, but the remains, excavated in 1942 by occupying German troops, now consist of little more than a massive paved terrace on which her shrine once stood. The lack of visible structures does not deter visitors from coming here, however, because the sheltered cove below the sanctuary site is excellent for swimming.

Áyios Ioánnis Church

An even less accessible site on the peninsula is the church of Áyios Ioánnis (St John), reached by means of a very rough track (the walk takes two to three hours) from Rodhopós. This is the route taken by thousands of pilgrims every year on 29 August (the feast of the birth of St John the Baptist) when boys sharing the name John (Ioánnis) are brought from all over the island for mass baptism. For the rest of the year this lonely shrine is deserted.

Goniás Monastery

Much closer to Kolimvári is the lovely Moní Goniás which dates mainly from its rebuilding in 1662, though it incorporates masonry of several periods. An early 17th-century stone balcony to the right of the gatehouse is supported on brackets carved with ferocious Venetian lions. Opposite the gatehouse is a Turkish fountain (1708), whose inscription reads: 'O flowing spring, pour water for me; water is vital to life, the sweetest element'. Through the gatehouse is the

The *Virgin and Child* icon in Moní Goniás is an aspect of special devotion

graceful monastic church containing fine examples of woodcarving, such as the abbot's chair.

Best of all are the outstanding 17th-century icons: those on the iconostasis of the central nave are the work of a Cretan monk called Parthenios. An icon in the north aisle (dated 1637 and signed by Konstantinou Paleokaia, also known as Palaiókapas) shows St Nicholas in bishop's robes seated on a scarlet cushion. Adjacent is an earlier work, the mid-15th-century figure of Christ as High Priest. The serene Virgin and Child in the south aisle is of the mid-17th-century period.

To the east of the church is a shady terrace with views to the distant hills of the Akrotíri peninsula. Embedded in the rear wall of the church is a cannon ball from the Turkish bombardment of 1866, when the monastery came under attack for its role in the rebellion against Turkish rule. To the left of the church is a small museum with an outstanding icon: *The Crucifixion* (1637), by Palaiókapas.
Goniás monastery; closed 12.30–4pm and all day Saturday.

MÁLEME

The German invasion of Crete began at Máleme on 20 May 1941 (see page 104), and today it is the site of the German War Cemetery. The cemetery stands on Hill 107 where much of the fighting took place and where many of the German paratroopers who took part in the airborne invasion were picked off with bullets as they floated to the ground. The statistics of the battle make grim reading and are a sober reminder that almost three times as many Germans died in the campaign as did Commonwealth troops (6,580 German troops killed or missing, compared with 2,000 on the Commonwealth side). The small pavilion at the entrance to the cemetery, with its map showing the progress of the battle, does not record how many Cretans suffered in this war – for it was they who bore the brunt of the awful reprisals taken by the Germans once the island was in their hands.

Today Hill 107 is a peaceful spot; the lower part is managed to encourage wildflowers in spring, and the upper part is packed with neat graves that spread all the way up to the hill crest. Here a terrace offers views over Máleme airstrip, the focus of the German assault and still in military use today.

Máleme is 16km west of Khaniá.

German war graves at Máleme

Nearby:

The countryside south of Máleme is dotted with small village churches which are far older than a first glance would suggest. Three in particular are worth a visit. Spiliá is reached by heading west to the Kolimvári crossroads, then south for 3km. Drive on through the village of Spiliá until you see a blue signpost pointing right to the church at the village exit. You first pass a little square on the right, shaded with plane trees and with a little gabled fountain in one corner. The church is another 500m on from the square, on a grassy mound to the right of a sharp bend. The simple building dates from the 12th century and the soot-blackened frescos inside from the 14th century. They depict scenes from the Life of the Virgin, including a lively Nativity with the Three Kings on the south wall, and the Presentation of Jesus in the Temple on the opposite wall.

Áyios Stéphanos

From Spiliá drive on south through Drakóna, then, after 1.5km, look for a

CYCLAMEN

Cyclamen creticum, found nowhere else in the world other than Crete, favours the island's shady gorges and scrubby woodland. Considerably smaller and less showy than its cultivated relatives, its delicate white flowers and leaves appear between March and May with the plant surviving and spreading underground by tubers outside this period.

white sign pointing right to Áyios Stéphanos church. This 10th-century building lies at the end of a delightful oak-shaded path renowned for the white cyclamen (see above) that flower on the left-hand bank in spring (these cyclamen – *Cyclamen creticum* – are most similar to *Cyclamen repandum* found on mainland Greece).

The walls of the ancient church are cracked and subsiding, but the 13th-century frescos remain clear enough for a Nativity scene to be made out, and, below it, the Stoning of St Stephen, the first Christian martyr, while next to both is a Pentecostal scene. Evangelists are painted round the tiny apse, but the scenes on the south wall are far more difficult to interpret.

Mikhaíl Arkhángelos

Just 1km further south a big sign points right to the extraordinary church of Mikhaíl Arkhángelos, known as the Rotonda because of its unusual central dome. From the outside this consists of a stepped series of concentric rings, diminishing in size as they climb upwards. Inside, the church resembles a beehive, with the side walls pierced by six tall arches, one of which frames the apse. On the floor there are the remains of 6th-century mosaics with a geometric pattern, while frescos of standing saints cover several walls.

The church is unique in its plan and shape, and archaeological excavations are in progress in and around the church, aimed at discovering more about its history. These suggest that the church is a rare survivor of the so-called First Byzantine period (mid-5th to mid-6th century), but with frescos from the 10th and 12th centuries.

THE BATTLE

The Battle of Crete took place over 50 years ago, but the events remain a talking point in the island's cafés to this very day and carefully tended war memorials are found on the main squares of almost every village on the island. These record the names of men, women and children, priests and abbots, shot in reprisal for Cretan acts of resistance during the war.

Churchill's plan

Churchill intended that Crete should be a safe haven for Allied troops driven south through Greece by the seemingly inexorable progress of German troops during the spring of 1941. He referred to Crete as an island fortress, believing that the British Mediterranean Fleet would be able to keep the Germans at bay, whilst the 32,000 British, Greek, Australian and New Zealand troops evacuated from Greece and the Balkans recouped their strength.

For a while this plan succeeded, and the Allied fleet drove off several attempts by German ships to invade the island. Frustrated, the Germans threw tens of thousands

OF CRETE

of troops into an airborne attack on Crete, which began on 20 May, 1941. Parachutists rained out of the sky over the Máleme airstrip (see page 108). Many were shot before they even touched down and others were killed by Cretan villagers, armed with primitive clubs and pitchforks, as they struggled to release themselves from their parachutes. For several hours the Allied troops beat off the attack, but, at a critical moment, poor communications led to Hill 107 being evacuated, and the Germans seized the advantage. With this hill secured, it was not long before German troop planes were landing at Máleme without resistance.

Cretans surrender to the Germans; many suffered brutal reprisals

to the southern shores of Crete where, under heavy aerial bombardment, ships took the troops off to the Egyptian port of Alexandria. It would have been a simple matter for the Germans to have halted this evacuation, if they had not been held up by an heroic regiment of Greek troops who defended a strategic river crossing for two whole days.

The evacuation

Realising that all was lost, Allied commanders concentrated on evacuating their weary troops from Crete as fast as possible. This involved an arduous trek through the White Mountains

Grim and heroic deeds marked the terrible Battle of Crete

The aftermath

German reprisals against the Cretan population for the troops lost in the invasion only served to increase resistance. Local people kept up relentless guerilla warfare against the invaders – at a heavy cost in terms of human life – for the whole duration of the war.

Moní Arkádhi church, with its baroque façade, has become a symbol of Cretan heroism

MONÍ ARKÁDHI

Moní Arkádhi has become a symbol of Cretan heroism in the cause of independence, a literal expression of the Cretan battle cry: 'Freedom or Death'. It was here that hundreds of resistance fighters blew themselves up rather than surrender to the Turks during the 1866–9 revolt. Huge numbers of people converge on the monastery every 9 November to commemorate the anniversary of the mass suicide.

The siege and its aftermath

The siege began on 7 November 1866, when Turkish soldiers surrounded the monastery. Hundreds of Cretan guerrillas had sought refuge inside, many of them with their wives and children.

The Turks eventually succeeded in demolishing the now-rebuilt gatehouse, and poured into the deserted monastery courtyard. On the instructions of Abbot Gabriel, the Cretan defenders had withdrawn to the now-roofless gunpowder store, which is to be found at the far left-hand side of the courtyard. Waiting until the very last minute, in order to trap and kill as many Turks as possible in the explosion, the abbot then gave the word for the powder kegs to be lighted. Nobody knows quite how many died – some say hundreds, others thousands. The event did, however, stir complacent politicians into action all around Europe. Until then, many powerful countries – Britain, France and Italy included – had stood by and ignored the atrocities being committed by the Turks in Crete. It took another 30 years before Crete gained a semblance of self-determination, but the events at Moní Arkhádi marked a significant turning point in the world's awareness of its plight.

Museum memorial

In the centre of the courtyard is the church with its fine baroque façade (dated 1587). To the right, the museum is full of mementoes of the siege: Turkish swords and cannon, portraits of some of those who died, the vestments of Abbot Gabriel, who led the heroic action against the siege, and – most poignant of all – the shrapnel-scarred and hand-painted banner of the stalwart Cretans who died in the defence of the monastery.

Moní Arkádhi is 26km southeast of Réthimnon.

Nearby:
Eléftherna

Eléftherna is the site of a fascinating post-Minoan hilltop town. Just beyond the village entrance sign, a concrete track leads downhill to the right (signposted 'To Ancientry' (sic)). This leads to a Roman villa built of materials salvaged from ancient Eléftherna – the sheer quantity of richly carved marble indicates the wealth of that city. Heading back up the idyllic gorge, you will pass a fine 10th-century church beside a spring. Back in the village turn right and follow signs to the Acropolis Taverna. Parking by the taverna, you can follow the track to the right that leads to the ancient hilltop city, poised on a knife-edge ridge between two deep gorges. The most prominent of the ruins is a late-Roman tower; note how the rock-cut path in front of it has been carved into a grid to resemble paving. A rock-cut path goes to the left of the tower and after some 300m runs out – turn left here and, immediately on the left, you will find a series of huge rock-cut cisterns, of cathedral-like proportions, cut into the cliffs below the city, and supported by a forest of pillars.

Eléftherna is another 39km to the east by road (10km by footpath).

Relic of the siege – a shrapnel-scarred icon in the monastic museum

The quiet and lonely Préveli monastery has often been at the centre of momentous events

MONÍ PRÉVELI

Moní Préveli enjoys an idyllic setting on the steep hills that sweep down to the Libyan Sea on the south of the island. One 19th-century traveller described the setting as a Cretan paradise, and 'one of the most happily chosen spots for a retreat from the cares and responsibilities of life'. In fact, Moní Préveli has seen more than its share of tumultuous events and is another of those monasteries that have played a conspicuous role in Cretan history.

Centre of resistance

The monastery was founded in the 16th century, on a site that lies further inland: the ruins of the original monastery still stand, alongside the Megapótomos river, on the road up to the present-day monastery. The monastery was moved to this more secluded position after the Turks took Crete. The new monastery, with its precious library, became a clandestine centre of learning under the Turkish occupation, and successive abbots took a leading role in organising

local revolts against the Turks.

From 1866 on, following the explosion that killed the rebels at Moní Arkádhi (see page 112), British sympathisers with the Cretan cause raised funds to buy a ship – the *Arkhadi*. This made regular trips to Crete, through the Turkish blockade, carrying weapons and supplies for the Cretan rebels, which were landed at the beach just to the east of this spot; again it was the monks of Moní Préveli who organised their distribution.

The Battle of Crete

Moní Préveli also played a key role in sheltering Commonwealth troops during the evacuation that took place at the end of the Battle of Crete in May 1941 (see page 110). The same beach below the monastery was used by the submarines that took troops off the island, landing them at the Egyptian port of Alexandria. A plaque in the monastery courtyard records the fact that hundreds of British, Australian and New Zealand soldiers were protected by the monks and guided to the beachhead from where they made their escape, all this 'in defiance of the ferocious reprisals suffered by the monks'.

The monastery today

Amongst the reprisals taken by the Germans was the partial destruction of the monastic complex. The monks themselves, however, had already destroyed what ancient building fabric and frescos had remained from the 17th century in their own rebuilding works in 1835. The buildings today are therefore relatively recent, but they make a harmonious ensemble. The church contains a splendidly carved and gilded iconostasis, covered in scenes from the Life of Christ. Some of these date from the mid-18th century, and have been transferred here from churches in the Préveli region to protect them from theft. The monastic museum is housed in the former stables where rock-cut mangers are now used as display cabinets. Exhibits include liturgical silver, and the vestments (dated 1701–10) of Abbot Jacob Préveli, the monastery's founder.

To Palm Beach

The little beach, which has so often featured in the history of Moní Préveli and Crete, lies to the east of the monastery, and can be reached from the monastic complex by means of a marked path. Allow at least half an hour and be prepared for some scrambling over steep and rocky terrain (for an alternative route see page 139). Provided that the beach is not too crowded, this can be a lovely spot.

The Megapótomos river flows into the sea at this point, and its banks are lined by groves of beautiful palm trees, the same rare Cretan native palms that grow

at Vái (see page 69). The whole estuary resembles a desert oasis, backed by the harsh rocks of the Kurtalióti ravine.

From the beach, you can continue eastwards, along rough tracks, for another 3km to the church of Ayiá Fotinis, one of numerous little churches lining this part of the southern coast. Ayía Fotinis dates from the late 14th century, and its walls feature frescos of the female saints, Fotiní, Marína, Paraskeví, Kyriakí and Eiríni.

Moní Préveli is 38km south of Réthimnon (see page 134 for a suggested route). Open: daily 9am–7pm, though the museum is closed from 2–3pm. Admission charge.

The Megapótomos river joins the sea at Préveli

PRIEST

Focus of learning and resistance

Cretans know the score and pretend a head-bowing deference to any monk that crosses their path. This exaggerated respect, afforded even by the most cynical of atheists, can be attributed to the key role played by the Greek Orthodox church during the dark years of the Turkish occupation, and again during the German occupation when the church served as the focal point for Cretan resistance. Priests and monks also ran clandestine schools under Turkish rule, in defiance of the ban on Christian education and worship, keeping alive the flame of

If your idea of a typical priest or monk is that of a humble, pious and charitable person, think again when it comes to Crete. Monks, especially, and many priests regard themselves as the aristocrats of the island and it is not unusual for them to treat those they consider their inferiors with a degree of arrogance that is quite untypical of Crete as a whole.

Greek nationalism. Great acts of heroism were committed by the predecessors of today's monks and priests. The major powers ignored the plight of Crete under the Turks until the rebels of Arkádhi monastery (see page 112) committed mass suicide in 1866. This event drew attention to Turkish brutality, galvanising Europe into belated action. Again, during World War II, the monks at Préveli

ND MONKS

monastery (see page 114) suffered vicious reprisals because of the help they gave to Allied troops escaping the island by submarine to Egypt.

Influence waning

For all this, memories of the past are beginning to fade and the influence of the church in the everyday life of the Cretan people is beginning to wane, at least in the urban centres. Even so, monks (who remain chaste) and priests (who are allowed to marry) are a highly visible presence in Cretan society, with their uncut locks and beards and their black cassocks, and no Cretan would consider an event in the life of the community complete – whether a school prize-giving or a wine festival – without the blessing and official presence of the clergy.

The flame of Greek nationalism is kept alive by the Orthodox church

PALAIÓKHORA

From being a small southern coast fishing village, Palaiókhora has recently expanded to become one of the island's most enjoyable up-market resorts. A huge new marina development is under construction that will add to the existing attractions but not – one hopes – destroy the authentic Cretan atmosphere that prevails here at the moment. That Cretan character extends to the fact that the town centre is virtually sealed off to traffic at night, when local people leaved their houses to play backgammon and drink *raki* outside the local tavernas, their chairs and tables filling the narrow streets.

Palaiókhora has two big beaches that can both be viewed from the castle that sits high above the town, built in 1279 by the Venetians and consisting now of little but the encircling walls. To the left

(east) of the town is the ferry harbour (see below) and then a huge sweep of mixed sand and shingle beach. To the right (west) is a huge beach of golden sand – flying its European Blue Flag (awarded to beaches that meet the highest standards of cleanliness) with pride. The waters on this side can be cold because of the mountain streams that pour into the bay to the west. In the height of summer this coolness can be welcome, though earlier in the year tends to deter all but the very hardiest of swimmers.

Offshore breezes make this a good spot for windsurfing too, and there is a hut at the far northwestern end of the beach where boards are available for hire.

Palaiókhora's Venetian castle rises above the ferry harbour

Walkers come to cool their feet in the crystal-clear waters of Soúyia Bay

South coast ferries

If you want a break from baking in the sun all day, you can take the south coast ferry from Palaiókhora's harbour and head along the coast, or across the Libyan Sea to the island of Gávdhos. Tickets and timetables are available from travel agents in the town, or from the ferry company kiosk on the harbour. The ferries operate between the beginning of April to the end of October. During this period there are daily services to the Elafonísi islands, to the west of Palaiókhora (see page 134), and eastwards to Soúyia (see below) and Ayía Rouméli (for the Samaria Gorge). Services to Gávdhos only operate at weekends (Friday, Saturday and Sunday from 1 April to 5 June, and in October; Friday, Saturday, Sunday and Monday from 6 June to 30 September).

Palaiókhora is 84km southwest of Khaniá.

Nearby:
Soúyia

Soúyia is where people who have walked the Samaria Gorge (see page 124) come by ferry to catch the bus back to Khaniá. In the height of summer, from lunchtime on, it can be very busy with hungry hikers enjoying a well-deserved meal in the several tavernas lining the shore. Once the walkers have gone, it reverts to being an almost deserted village with a broad pebbly, beach and views to distant Gávdhos. Across the beach, to the east, you can make out the remains of the ancient Roman port of Elyros either side of a small river estuary. To the west of the village, a well-marked path (very steep in places) makes for the ruins of a 4th-century BC temple to Asklepios (god of healing) at Lisós, some 3km across the cliffs.

Gávdhos

Gávdhos island is worth a trip if you want to say that you have stood on the most southerly point in Europe. The island is about two hours south of Crete by ferry, and the day-trip allows you four hours to explore the tiny harbour at Karabé or walk inland to the main village of Kastrí (where there is precious little to see). Local people have taken to meeting the ferry and providing transport to the island's best beaches, which lie to the north, or to the southernmost tip of the island, and of Europe, Tripití point.

Réthimnon

*R*éthimnon is a very likeable town from which vehicles have largely been excluded, leaving the narrow streets to the bustling hubbub of human traffic. Watching the parade of people up and down the main street is an enthralling pastime, especially from the comfort of one of the numerous pavement cafés clustering round the Rimóndi Fountain. The shopping is excellent (if more expensive than Khaniá) and the town remains essentially Cretan, with traditional boot-makers and ironmongers selling axes and sickles mixed in amongst the tourist shops selling embroidery, lace and T-shirts.

Another feature of the city is its architecture, a legacy of Venetian rule. Look up in almost any street and you are sure to see ornamental balconies and elaborate window frames above the modern shopfronts. Look down alleys and you will see doorways carved with coats of arms, cherubs, vines or crouching lions, or crumbling façades propped up by timber buttresses waiting to be restored.

RÉTHIMNON ARCHAEOLOGICAL MUSEUM

Réthimnon's new Archaeological Museum is housed within one of the defensive bastions opposite the main gate of the Venetian Fort (see page 122). Light floods into the museum from its central atrium, around which are top-

Réthimnon's café-lined Venetian Harbour is the centre of the city's bustling nightlife

RÉTHIMNON TOWN PLAN

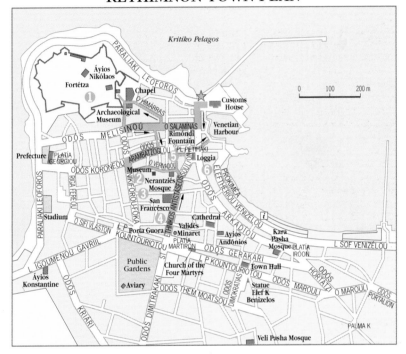

Kritiko Pelagos

Áyios Nikólaos
Fortétza
Chapel
Archaeological Museum
Customs House
Venetian Harbour
O SALAMINAS
Rimóndi Fountain
PL PETIHAKI
Loggia
Prefecture
PLATIA GEORGIOU
ODÓS KORONEOU
RIGA FEREOU
Museum
Nerantziés Mosque
San Francésco
PARALIAKI LEOFOROS
Stadium
Cathedral
Validés Minaret
PLATIA MARTIRON
Porta Guora
Kara Pasha Mosque
PLATIA IROON
L SOF VENIZELOU
Áyios Andónios
Public Gardens
Church of the Four Martyrs
Town Hall
Statue Elef K Benizelos
Áyios Konstantine
Aviary
Veli Pasha Mosque
PALMA K

0   100   200 m

displays of sculpture, funerary chests, coins, pottery and jewellery from excavations in Réthimnon province.

Minoan crafts

The museum provides an excellent introduction to all the various crafts practised by the Minoans. Here you will find beautiful and delicate pottery that would not look out of place on a modern dinner table. From various caves and peak sanctuaries in the province there are clay figures of priestesses and bulls. There is also a large display of clay *larnakes* (burial chests) painted with abstract renderings of sea creatures, such as octopuses, fish and nautilus shells.

Others depict lively hunting scenes, suggesting that the Minoan countryside was alive with deer, wild horned goats and flowers.

The dead were placed in these *larnakes*, trussed up tight in the foetal position, knees to chin, and the chests were then placed in chambered tombs. Some *larnakes* have a hole in the base, which has led some archaeologists to suggest that they may have been used as domestic bathtubs before being re-deployed as tomb chests. Such an explanation seems a touch far-fetched, as do the tortuous attempts of Minoan archaeologists to prove that the sacred double axe symbol – the *labrys* – bears a

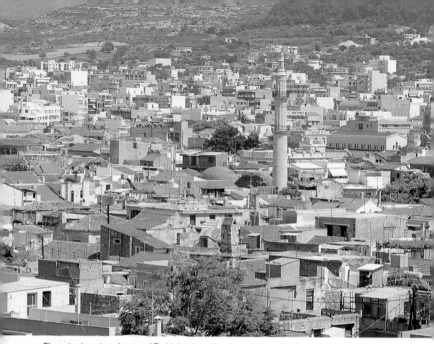

Elegant minarets, a legacy of Turkish rule, point skyward from Réthimnon's close-packed city centre

geometrical relationship to the form of the labyrinth, the maze-like pattern that appears on coinage of the Hellenistic period (from the 6th century BC). Examples of both coins and axes are displayed here, so you can make up your own mind.

Statuary

Finally there is an unusually good display of Graeco–Roman statuary, including a very fine bronze helmeted youth (probably Mercury) salvaged from a Roman ship wrecked off Ayía Galíni. Nearby is a statue of Aphrodite, goddess of love and beauty, and another of the Empress Faustina, wife of the emperor Antoninus Pius (AD110–40).

Opposite the main entrance to the Venetian Fortress. Tel: 0831-29975. Open: Monday 11am–5pm; Tuesday to Friday, 8am–5pm; Saturday and Sunday 8.30am–3pm. Admission charge.

VENETIAN FORTRESS (ALSO KNOWN AS THE FORTÉTZA)

Réthimnon's massive fortress dominates distant views of the town and seems big enough to accommodate the whole population of Réthimnon in times of trouble. It is said to be the biggest Venetian fortress ever built and the impressive walls encompass churches, an open-air theatre and a whole network of underground magazines and cisterns, as well as ruined accommodation blocks for garrison troops. A climb through the pine-planted interior is worthwhile just for the views, especially at sunset. Alternatively, you can watch day turn to night from the Sunset taverna, which sits on the coastal road, below the west-facing fortress walls.

The marvellous views emphasise the strategic value of this particular headland, and its fortress was built in 1573, specifically as a base from which to

VENETIAN RULE

The Venetians changed the face of Réthimnon and the whole of Crete during the 465 years of their rule (1204–1669). Venice acquired the island by questionable means (as part of the spoils of the Fourth Crusade) but compensated by building the harbours, shipyards, fortresses, palaces and public buildings that now grace the island's principal cities. At first, Venetian rule was exploitative; timber was stripped from the hillsides, heavy taxes imposed and Christianity was forced on the Cretan people, whipping up resentment amongst the Orthodox clergy. In time, however, a more fruitful relationship evolved, with Cretans and Venetians intermarrying and sending their children to Italy to be educated. As a result, the arts flourished in the 16th and 17th centuries, the period known as the Cretan Renaissance. This was the era that produced Mikhaíl Damaskinós, the great icon painter (see page 38) and the even more famous El Greco (see page 36).

Even greater things might have been achieved but for the Turkish siege of Iráklio that began in 1647. Remarkably, Cretans and Venetians, fighting side by side, held off the siege for 22 years, and the Turkish commander, Hussein Pasha, was recalled to Istanbul and publicly executed for his failure to take the island. Lack of support from other European powers eventually led to the collapse of Venetian resistance, leaving the Turks to take the island in 1669, beginning a period of cultural and economic stagnation for the Cretans under their loathed Islamic rulers.

Beneath the walls of the Fortétza

stamp out piracy. In this it succeeded, but the fortress did not prove much of a defence when the Turks arrived in 1645, seizing the city after a siege of only 23 days – a mere trifle compared with Iráklio's 21-year stand-off. The Turks built the big domed mosque that is the most prominent building in the interior of the fortress today.

Odós Salaminos. Open: daily 8am–8pm. Admission charge.

SAMARIA GORGE (FARANGI SAMARIAS)

After Knosós, the Samaria Gorge is the best-known attraction on Crete, and every summer tens of thousands of people trudge the 15km-long path that follows the bottom of the gorge, finding none of the tranquillity and solitude that one normally associates with walking in the countryside. If you hate crowds, set out early in the day (the gorge opens at 6am) or walk one of Crete's other, equally spectacular, ravines (see page 144).

The gorge is only open from the beginning of May to the end of October

Pausing for thought and refreshment at the bottom of the Samaria Gorge

because flash floods are a very real danger in the rainy season.

There is no road access to the southern end, so your only way back is by ferry (to Soúyia, Palaiókhora or Khóra Sfakíon), or by retracing your steps up the gorge (there are rooms to rent in Ayía Rouméli, at the southern end of the gorge, so it is perfectly feasible to do this over two days).

The times of ferries and connecting buses can be checked at one of Crete's tourist information centres (the times

vary according to the season). Of course, you can leave the logisitics of getting to and from the gorge to somebody else by signing up for a coach excursion, though this means setting out with a crowd of 30 or more people. You can also hire a taxi to get you there and arrange to be collected at Ayía Rouméli. One or two taxis are available for hire in Ayía Rouméli itself, and they will take you back to Khaniá or anywhere else on the island – provided you get to them before someone else does. If all else fails, there are plenty of rooms for rent in Soúyia, Palaiókhora and Khóra Sfakíon, where you can spend the night.

In the gorge

The total length of the gorge is 13km, and it is another 2km to the coastal village of Ayía Rouméli with kilometre posts marking out the route. You should allow at least five hours to do the walk. Keep your entrance ticket as you will be asked to hand it in at the exit – this is a simple device to help the park wardens count the number of people in the gorge, and send in the rescue services, if necessary, to locate stranded walkers. You should take sufficient food and drink to sustain you along the route (there are tavernas at either end, but not within the gorge itself). Drinking water is supplied from taps at six points along the gorge, four of which also have toilets.

The Lazy Way

If you do not feel like tackling the whole gorge, there are two alternatives. One is to walk the first 2km or so from the northern end of the gorge; this is exhilarating, because the route plunges some 900m down the so-called Xylóskalo ('Wooden Staircase'), through beautiful pine woods; the obvious drawback is that

you have to climb all the way back up, and 900m of staircase is no joke.

The other option, known as 'The Lazy Route', is to tackle the gorge from the southern end. Despite the name, this involves a stiff uphill climb to the gorge entrance (2km), followed by a walk of about 4km through the narrowest part of the gorge, where the path is squeezed between towering cliffs, up to 600m high. You can go all the way up to the gorge's most famous landmark, the so-called Iron Gates (Sidherespórtes), where the sides of the gorge close in to leave a gap of a mere 3m. To get here involves a there-and-back walk of about 11km, so you might just as well walk the whole gorge.

The Samaria Gorge begins 43km south of Khaniá, on the Omalós Plateau, and runs southwards to end 2km north of Ayía Rouméli. Admission charge.

Despite the crowds, nothing detracts from the adventure of walking the gorge

THE VÁMOS PENINSULA

The Vámos peninsula east of Khaniá has recently been 'discovered' by up-market tour operators, so that its coastal villages – Kalíves, Almyrída and Yeoryióupoli – are beginning to develop a rash of new villa complexes around their margins. For the present, they remain unspoiled, and they make an excellent base from which to explore western Crete by car.

Yeoryióupoli

Yeoryióupoli is named after Prince George, son of the King of Greece, who was appointed High Commissioner of Crete from 1898 to 1906, ruling the island in the interim period when Crete still technically belonged to Turkey, but enjoyed a measure of autonomy. The prince used to enjoy coming here for the hunting, and the area is still renowned for its birdlife. The Vrýsanos river flows into the sea at this point, and the marshy margins of the river are a haven for birds, as well as for freshwater crabs, terrapins, frogs and fish. Locally the Vrýsanos is known as the 'Turtle River' (sometimes marked on maps as Almirós), and you can hire pedal boats at the village's fishing harbour for exploring its reed-fringed banks.

Yeoryóupoli also sits on the western edge of a huge and often deserted sandy beach that spreads for 12km in the direction of Réthimnon.

Vríses and Samonás

Another attractive feature of the village is the wonderful green avenue of giant eucalyptus trees that forms the old road out of the village (once the main road, but now superseded by the National Highway). Following this will bring you to pretty Vríses, famous for its creamy yoghurt and wild honey, and on to Néo Khorió. Here it is well worth diverting to Samonás for Crete's most appealingly sited church. If you want to go inside the church, call at the house of the guardian, which is on the left at the village exit. The guardian or his wife will come with you and open up the church. Just beyond the village you will catch your first glimpse of the church (see page 83), beautifully sited on a knoll in a lovely green valley, with no other building in sight. Built of honey-coloured stone, with a tall central dome, the church dates from the 11th century, and the frescos inside, including a tender Virgin and Child, date from 1230–6.

Yeoryióupoli is one of several up-market resorts on the Vámos peninsula

The ruined hilltop city of Áptera against the backdrop of the White Mountains

Áptera

After the detour to Samonás, the road through Stílos passes a turning, just before Megála Khoráfia, that leads to the ruined hilltop city of Áptera. The extent of the overgrown ruins indicates just how large this post-Minoan city was. Its exact foundation date is not known, but it was flourishing in the 7th century BC and was occupied until the Arab conquest of Crete in AD824. The walls can be traced for a circuit of some 4km, but the most obvious remains are those of the Turkish-era fortress, standing at the highest point on the hill, and offering extensive views over the Vámos peninsula and Soúdha Bay. Also visible is a Venetian fort on a prominent hill to the north – this is now used as a prison.

Beaches and wildflowers

Kalíves and Almyrída, both on the western edge of the Vámos peninsula, have sandy, gently shelving beaches, perfectly safe for children to play on. Beyond here, a network of narrow lanes threads the peninsula, well worth exploring if you are interested in wildflowers. The northern and eastern edges of the peninsula are stony and exposed to wind, so hundreds of tiny fields have been created by clearing the soil and using the rock to form drystone walls. Stone-paved paths thread their way between the walls, and some fields, no longer cultivated, have been re-colonised by masses of flowers, including wild lupins.

If your explorations take you through the village of Gavalokhóri, stop to look at the little museum, reached up the lane opposite the war memorial. This contains miscellaneous objects collected by the villagers, from old photographs to weapons from World War II.

Yeoryióupoli lies 33km east of Khaniá, 26km west of Réthimnon.

Khaniá

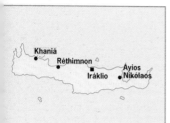

This walk introduces you to the intricate maze of narrow alleys in the old city and harbour area (for map of route see page 96). *Allow 1 hour – but longer if you are tempted to browse in some of Khaniá's best shops .*

Start at the elegant cross-shaped **market hall (1)**, an elegant neo-classical building of 1911, packed with good things to buy for picnics or presents. From the newspaper kiosk at the centre of the market, head west, past the fish stalls, and exit from the building down the café-lined flight of steps. Turn right then first left into Odós Skridlóf, known as 'Leather Alley' for obvious reasons – bags, belts and sandals are hung from the shop awnings in such profusion that it is impossible to proceed at anything other than browsing pace. The prices here are very keen; the only problem is too much choice!

Once through Skridlóf, turn right down Odós Khalídon

Khaniá's captivating
harbour

passing the cathedral, the **Church of Three Martyrs (2)**, on the right. Although it has a pleasing façade this church is disappointingly modern within. Genuinely ancient, by contrast, is the former **Turkish Baths (3)**, further down on the right, topped by 12 domes sitting like a dozen eggs in a box. Part of the bathhouse is now used as a bronze-workers' foundry. Further down on the left, is the **Archaeological Museum (4)**, housed in the former Franciscan church (see page 94), with the stumpy remains of a Gothic campanile (belltower) to the left of the façade.

Beyond the museum is the café-lined Platía Santriváni, a lively spot at night when buskers and street traders set up their pitch. Just before the square, turn left into Odós Zambelioú, a typical street in the old city, crammed with characterful shops and old Venetian town houses, some shored up and awaiting restoration.

Just where the street narrows and begins to climb, look for Odós Moschón, an alley on the right that leads down to the **Renieri Gate (5)**, with its family coat of arms and inscriptions dating the fine classical gateway to 1608. Through the gate, immediately on the left, is the late 15th-century chapel of the Renieri family, whose town house (now Sultana's restaurant) stands alongside. Ahead, at the end of Odós Moschón, there are several more elegant Venetian palaces, some now converted to up-market hotels.

Turn right beside the medieval style jettied-out façade of the Hotel Contessa, then left up steps beside the Amphora Hotel, pausing at the top to admire the jumble of picturesque alleys that intersect at this photogenic spot. Go straight across, then right down Odós A Gampá. Another fine Venetian palace (now the

In the maze of narrow shop-lined streets of the old Venetian city

Eugenia II Hotel) with ornate stone balconies and window decoration, terminates the street. Turn right here, down Odós Ageloú to reach the entrance to the Naval Museum (see page 97) set in the restored 16th-century Venetian fortress known as the **Firkás (6)**. From the walls of the Fortress (no charge for entry) there are sweeping views of the whole harbour, with its lighthouse, sea wall, arsenal and domed Mosque of the Janissaries (see page 94).

To return to the market, follow the harbour back round to Platía Santriváni, then retrace your steps up Odós Khalídon.

Réthimnon

Réthimnon is tailor-made for strolling, with its narrow traffic-free streets, tempting shop displays and traditional architecture. To make the most of this walk, come at dusk, when the sunset views from the Fortétza are stunning (for map of route see page 121). *Allow 1 hour.*

Start at the Customs House end of the **Venetian Harbour** where the fishermen gather to mend their nets. There is a small fish market here most mornings, opposite Benetsianíko's bar, and there is also a good view of the 16th-century Venetian lighthouse. Turning your back to the harbour, take the road to the left, then second right (Odós Salamínas), then second right (Odós Himárras). This road leads up to the Fortétza, passing first the Centre of Contemporary Art which, despite its name,

exhibits the work of 18th and 19th-century Greek artists. The whole area around the museum is developing as a centre for young artisans and you can see jewellers, icon painters and potters at work as you stroll. The road ends at the entrance to the Archaeological Museum, on the right (see page 120), and the **Fortétza (1)** on the left (see page 122).

Coming out of the Fortétza, head straight down the steep cobbled ramp that leads to Odós Melisinoú, turn left and then second right (Odós Xanthoúdidou) beside the Fortezza Hotel. By night this narrow street, and all the others in the vicinity, is packed with taverna tables. By day, shops selling glass, jewellery and colourful beachwear catch the eye as you take the second right (Odós Arambatzoglóu) and follow it to the little square at the top.

Turn left here (Odós Nikiforoú-Fóka), then second left, into Odós Vernadóu. This street has many fine

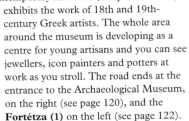

Left: Turkish-style balconies shade the streets
Right: the Venetian lighthouse

houses in the Venetian architectural style, including the grand palazzo, halfway down on the right, that is being restored to form a new home for the **History and Folk Art Museum (2).** A short distance further down is the elegant Odeion concert hall, better known as the **Nerantziés Mosque (3)**. Originally built as a church in the mid-16th century, it was converted to a mosque in 1657 and given its stylish minaret in 1890. Today the building is used for concerts and theatrical performances.

At the end of Odós Vernadóu, turn right into the city's crowded main street, Odós Ethníkos Antístáseos. Walk up the street to explore the fascinating range of shops and the market at the far end, up against the 16th-century Porta Guora, all that remains of the Venetian city walls. Coming back down the street, take the third left (Odós Áyios Fragkískou) for a look at the fine gateway of the 16th-century **Franciscan friary (4)**, now a school. Cafés dominate this end of the street and cluster thickly around the **Rimóndi Fountain (5)**. Built in 1629, it has four lions' heads spouting water into a marble basin.

To the right of the fountain, Odós Paleológou contains the 16th-century **Loggia (6)**, another relic of Venetian rule, built as a covered market but now sadly disused.

From here it is a short step down Odós Nearhoú back to the harbour.

The Thériso Gorge (Farangi Thérissiano)

This undemanding circular route is an appetiser for more ambitious drives. If you have come to Crete mainly to laze on the beach, consider doing this particular drive, at least, to sample a Byzantine frescod church and one of Crete's several deep ravines.
Allow 2–3 hours.

From the centre of Khaniá, follow signs for Kastélli. After 3km you will pass a left-turn signposted Thériso – ignore this and take the next left turn, at the traffic lights, signposted Omalós. Follow the flat road through orange groves (heady with scent in April and May). After 14km you will reach a major junction with a petrol station at a spot known as Mnimeio. Next to this, hidden in a pine grove, is a grim war memorial with a glass altar displaying the skulls of Cretan resistance fighters shot by German firing squads.

Take the right turn (signposted Alikianós/Soúyia), crossing over the river Kerítis. On entering Alikianós village turn right, then almost immediately right again, following the signs for Koufós. After 300m you will pass Áyios Yeíryios church. Take the next right and continue for 1km until you see a red and white sign pointing right for Áyios Cyrgiánnis church, completely hidden amongst orange groves. This lovely 14th-century church has lost its dome but this allows light in so that you can study the frescos of serene saints (painted around 1430), and the two re-used 6th-century pillars and capitals to the north of the crossing.

Go back to the petrol station, this time turning right for Fournés, passing through more citrus groves with good views of the Levká Óri (White Mountains) ahead, then climbing gently

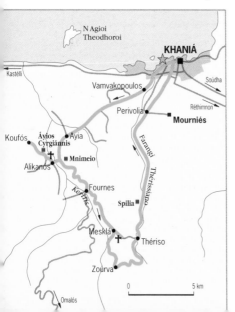

Pausing to let the ubiquitous sheep and goats of Crete pass to their grazing grounds

up a winding river valley dotted with plane trees, oaks and sweet chestnuts.

In Fournés, take the left fork to Mesklá along a narrow, winding mountain road. On entering Mesklá, look for the track on the left, just after the bridge, that leads up to a 14th-century church with well preserved frescos in the nave (dated 1303) and in the entrance narthex (mid-15th century).

Carry on up through the village for a short, but adventurous, drive of 11km on an unmetalled track through Zoúrva to Thériso. The road is perfectly feasible in a hired car so long as you take it at a measured pace.

Thériso marks the start of the scenic Thériso Gorge, whose sheer craggy cliffs tower either side of the road that weaves along the bottom, crossing the river again and again via numerous stone bridges. After 6km, the road passes beneath a huge cave set in the base of a cliff, with house-sized boulders strewn about the valley floor. You can stop here to listen to

the music of sheep bells echoing across the sides of the gorge and to enjoy the rich and varied wildflowers. Continue on to the end of the gorge, after which it is just 10km, on the same road, back to Khaniá.

THE MESKLA REBELS

Mesklá was the base for a rebellion against Venetian rule in the 16th century. Rebel leader, George Kandanoleon, ran a rival administration, refusing to pay taxes, until he foolishly sought to make his rule legitimate by marrying his son to the daughter of a Venetian aristocrat. Kandanoleon and his supporters celebrated the marriage in typical Cretan style. When they were all stupefied with food and drink, Venetian troops rounded them all up and either shot them on the spot, or hanged them in surrounding villages as a grim warning.

The Elafonísi Islands

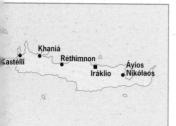

The unspoiled islands and beaches at the south-western edge of Crete are difficult to reach and this drive involves covering long distances on unmetalled roads – perfectly feasible at a steady pace (but don't set out without checking that all your tyres, including the spare, are sound). *Allow all day.*

From Kastélli Kissámou take the westward road to Plátanos. Take the right turn to Falásarna (see page 103) to visit the ruins of the 4th-century BC port. Otherwise continue through this rather dusty and unattractive village on the Sfinári road. The route now passes through scenic hills with the sea always in view. You will glimpse endless rows of plastic tunnels and greenhouses down on the fertile plain below. Growing bananas and out-of-season salad vegetables for export to the Greek mainland is a major industry.

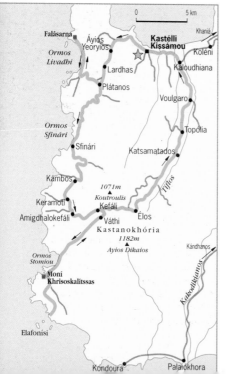

After Kámbos, set in its wooded green valley, the metalled surface gives way to a good, level, wide dirt track. After Keramotí, sweeping views open up to the right over Stómiou Bay (Ormos Stómiou). At Kefáli, turn right immediately after driving through the village, following the sign to Khrisoskalítisses ('Golden Stair').

The reason for the name may become apparent once you reach the beautiful white-walled convent with its powder-blue roofs. The convent is set on a sheer-sided rocky outcrop with steps (*skali* in Greek) leading down to a cove. One of the 90 steps is said to be made of gold (*khrisos*), but only those who are free from sin are able to see it! There has been a hermitage here since at least the 13th century. The present buildings were constructed in the mid-19th century and once supported a community of 200 – now reduced to just two.

From here, the last 5km of track to Elafonísi are bumpy and potholed – great

Above: Keramotí village
Right: the Elafonísi Islands, reached by wading

care is needed to avoid damaging your tyres. Your destination is an idyllic beach, still remote enough not to have been spoiled (though there are simple tavernas and rooms to rent here) with warm clear water, shells, rock pools and darting fish. The sea is shallow enough (less than a metre deep at the maximum) that you can wade to the nearest offshore island to another lovely tree-shaded beach. How long the area will remain unspoiled is open to question. New roads are being opened up east to Palaiókhora, and there are plans for a big resort hotel.

For now, however, you must return along the dirt track to Kefáli, turning right to pick up the metalled road to Élos. Élos is the capital of the region known as the Kastanokhória – the Chestnut Villages – because sweet chestnuts are grown here as a commercial crop (their harvesting is celebrated by a chestnut festival in late October). Come here in July and the air will be thick with the scent of chestnut blossom. In early November the trees turn golden and in late April the fresh new leaf buds unfurl.

Shortly after Katsamatados, woodland gives way to the cliffs and caves of the Topólia Gorge. After this last burst of excitement, the road descends rapidly to Kaloudhiana, where you should turn left to return to Kastélli, or right to join the Khaniá highway at Koléni.

The Amári Valley

The Amári Valley is rich in Byzantine churches which provides an excuse to explore an area rich in spring wildflowers and little visited by other tourists. Most churches are open all the time (if not, ask for the key in the nearest *kafeníon*). Take a torch for illuminating the frescos. *Allow at least half a day.*

From Réthimnon, follow the Old Road east along the seafront until you come to Perivolia, then turn right (signposted Amári) to pass under the National Highway. Shortly afterwards, turn right to Khromonastíri. Just before the village, look for a left turn signposted to Áyios Eftíkhios, down a rough 2km-long

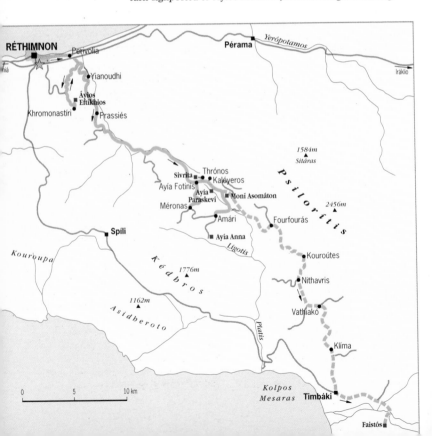

track. The domed church has frescos dating back to the 12th century – thus making them amongst the earliest to survive on Crete.

Back on the Amári road, continue to Ayía Fotinís, turning right at the village junction. As you drive through the village, the broad Amári valley is revealed to the left. In Méronas look for the church of the Panayía on the left just after the village war memorial. The jumble of frescos here date from 1339. The delicate icon of the Virgin is late 14th century, and one of the oldest on Crete.

Backtrack now to Ayía Fotinís and turn left immediately after the village exit to Thrónos. The tiny church in the village centre, with its Venetian-influenced Gothic portal, has 14th-century frescos of the Life of the Virgin in the apse and later 15th-century frescos in the same theme in the nave. Remains of a geometric mosaic continue from the interior to the outside of the church running up to the excavated footings of its much larger 4th-century predecessor. Further down the village street, a concrete path on the left to Sívrita (signposted Sýbritos) leads uphill to the recently excavated site of the ancient Amári Valley capital, founded around the 5th century bc and still inhabited into the early medieval period.

Return to the main road, and about 2km further on (1.5km beyond the left turn to Kalóyeros), park on the right and look down into the valley for the domed church of Ayía Paraskeví, set among the fields beside two cypress trees. This church contains the grave of Yeóryios Khortátzis, a 15th-century local clan leader. A much decayed fresco depicts him in armour on horseback taking leave of his wife to fight against the Venetians. This little church was attached to Moní Asomáton monastery, which stands at the

The unspoilt hilltop town of Amári overlooks its own fertile valley

crossroads some 3km further down the road. The walled and fortified monastery is now used as an agricultural college, but nobody objects if you go in to the courtyard to look at the 15th-century church whose furnishings are now in the Historical Museum of Crete in Iráklio (see page 36).

Turn right in front of the monastery and drive to Amári, the modern valley capital. Immediately on entering the village, turn right opposite the police station, following the downhill road to Ayía Anna. The damaged frescos in the apse contain an inscription dating them to 1225, making them the oldest firmly dated frescos on Crete. Emerging from the church there are splendid views across the valley to the mighty Psilorítis range rising like a cliff. Amári, an unspoilt hilltop town, offers a chance to stop and soak up the rural atmosphere before heading back the way you came to Réthimnon, or heading on south, via Timbáki, to the cluster of archaeological sites around Faistós (see pages 44 and 88).

The Kurtalióti Ravine (Farangi Kourtaliotiko)

This short but rewarding drive will take you through a ravine, reminiscent of the famous Samaria Gorge, to Moní Préveli, the monastery overlooking the Libyan Sea. Take respectable clothes for admission to the monastery but plan to leave them off if you visit the nearby beaches. *Allow at least half a day.*

Take the road south out of Réthimnon, past the public gardens, signposted to Spíli. After 8km, turn right at the signpost to the Late Minoan Cemetery of Arméni *(open 8.30am–3pm daily except Monday)*. Here are numerous rock-cut tombs dating to the late second millennium BC. The site is covered in orchids and anemones in spring.

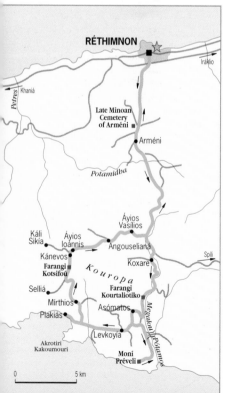

Back on the main road continue for 12km and take the right turn, signposted to Plakiás/Préveli Monastery. Soon you will turn a corner to find yourself in the Kurtalióti Ravine, passing beneath sheer cliffs with the Megapótomos (literally 'Big River') to your left. Part way down the ravine on the left is a layby. If you pull in here you will experience the breeze that gives the ravine its name ('Windy Gorge') whilst looking up at the cliff faces, pitted with caves and as brown as raw cork bark.

At the southern end of the short ravine, enter Asómatos then turn left for Moní Préveli and left again. About 2km beyond this last turning you will pass a cooling spot where walkers dip their feet in the Megapótomos near to a pretty 19th-century bridge and just before the ruins of the original 16th-century monastery. Its successor, built in the 17th century, lies 4km further along the narrow winding road on a clifftop terrace with far-

Above: Plakiás makes a good spot for lunch
Left: crossing the ravine

Plakiás. Beyond Levkoyía, tracks lead left down to a series of pretty coves backed by caves where nobody seems to bother much about wearing any clothes. Plakiás itself sits in a lovely sheltered bay with sweeping views and there is a good choice of beachside places to eat and drink to be had.

To return to Réthimnon, drive out of Plakiás on the road that brought you in and turn left after 1km for Mírthios, a pretty village clinging to the mountains overlooking the sea. At the next junction go straight on (not left to Selliá), driving up the steep-sided Kotsiphós Gorge. At the next junction go straight on (ignoring the left turn to Káli Sikía).

From Áyios Ioánnis onwards the road passes through delightful wooded country where cypress trees shade sheep-grazed pastures cut by streams. Just after Áyios Vasílios, turn left to rejoin the main Réthimnon road.

reaching views to the sea (for the monastery and its museum see page 114).

Driving back to the bridge, a driveable track leads right and along the river to the so-called Palm Beach (see page 115) but this can be crowded. Other beaches are found by continuing back the way you came and turning left, following signs to

The Ímbros Gorge (Farangi Ímvrotiko)

If you are not up to walking the Samaria Gorge (or if it is closed when you visit Crete) there are several possible substitutes, including this lazy way of enjoying the Ímbros Gorge by car. *Allow at least half a day.*

Coming from either Khaniá or Réthimnon, take the well-signposted turning off the National Highway to Vríses (see page 126). This attractive town is the meeting point of five roads, and is a popular stopping-off point for hungry travellers. Follow signposts to Khóra Sfakíon through the town and soon you will start to climb towards the Levká Óri (White Mountains).

After 5km turn left (signposted Alíkambos) and, less than 1km on, look for a graffiti-covered concrete embankment on a right-turning bend, and turn left down a track to the church of

the Panayía. Numerous springs gush out of the hillside and they are channelled into a 16th-century Venetian cistern (restored 1909). A grassy downhill track to the left leads to the church, idyllically set in an orange grove. The frescos (dated 1315) are some of the best preserved in Crete and depict biblical scenes, from Adam and Eve to the Nativity and Crucifixion (if the church is locked, the friendly priest can usually be found tending the modern church in Alíkambos, further up the road).

Go back to the main road and turn left, passing through the barren rocky landscape around Krapis. Some 5km further on, the scenery changes as you look down to your left, into a neat patchwork of tiny fields with a cone-shaped hill crowned by a circular Turkish fortress. Ímbros village marks the beginning of the gorge. From the road you will see little of its stern majesty

Above: the road follows the clifftops above the gorge. Right: the castle at Frangokástello

unless you pull over at one of the numerous view points along the route. The road winds round the top of the cliffs high above the western edge of the gorge. You can, however, descend into the gorge on foot from Ímbros village, following the well-signposted footpath (if you want to walk the whole route, allow 3 hours to reach its southern end, and either check the times of return buses before you set out, or arrange for a taxi to collect you).

The road now descends via a series of hairpin bends with far reaching views to Khóra Sfakion (see page 104), an attractive fishing village where you can enjoy lunch in a taverna set by the side of the crystal-clear sea. The beach here is of shingle – if you fancy a swim, head east on the broad flat coast road to Frangokástello, where there is a gently shelving child-friendly beach of golden sand and an almost intact 14th-century

beachside castle to explore.

For a completely different experience, head east out of Khóra Sfakíon on the vertiginous road to Anópoli, turning left at the village taverna to follow the new road (not yet shown on many maps) to the village of Arádena. This village, set high above a spectacular ravine, was abandoned some years ago. Left to crumble, the village and surrounding fields give a real sense of Cretan village life as it was before the age of concrete and plastic.

The Cretan Shepherd

Drive along any rural road in Crete and it will not be long before you encounter a flock of sheep or goats with an attendant shepherd, probably seated nearby beneath the shade of an olive tree. Stop on any rural road and you will hear the musical clamour of bells. Traditionally, long bells are hung round the necks of goats and wide ones round sheep, with seven different sizes and notes so that the shepherd can identify each individual in his flock. The shepherd who spends his lifetime looking after these hardy foragers will probably be dressed in a fine pair of knee boots, baggy Cretan pantaloons and lace headcap if he is over 40 years of age, and nearby will be a donkey carrying a wooden pack saddle and panniers.

Times are changing, however, and younger shepherds are more likely to be dressed in jeans and trainers and driving a pick-up truck. Regardless of age, all shepherds carry a crook, whose shape varies from region to region.

Shepherding is a hard and lonely life and although both lamb and *feta* cheese are staples of the Cretan diet, it is rare to find a wealthy farmer – one reason why fewer and fewer young people take up shepherding, aspiring instead to a more comfortable office job.

The lonely figure of a shepherd searching for green pastures

GETTING AWAY FROM IT ALL

'Crete is a continent.'
J GAITANIDES

Walking on Crete

*U*ntil the 1970s, Crete had almost no roads, a situation, in Cretan eyes, brought about by their Turkish rulers who deliberately suppressed the island's economy and made no investment in infrastructure. Instead, the island was covered in a network of tracks connecting one village with the next, along which goods were transported by donkey.

Supplementing these medieval roads were footpaths, called *kalderími*, paved with the local stone and usually sheltered from the sun by high walls to either side. Where these footpaths survive they nearly always serve to link one church to the next, or a village to its fields, and the walls support a wide variety of plant life.

Walking in Crete is a matter of seeking out the vestiges of this medieval network, something that is becoming increasingly difficult to do as *kalderími* become choked with scrub from lack of use, and as tracks are concreted over or tarmacked for the benefit of motorists.

Guides and equipment
The presence of tarmac very much depends upon the wealth of the local

Walking the Kurtalióti Ravine: the ruined monastery at Moní Préveli

community: each village pays to have its own roads metalled and, inevitably, it is the poorer inland regions where the tracks survive and where the walking is best. These are also remote regions where help is a long way off if you get into trouble, so basic precautions are essential. Do not set out without telling someone (such as your hotel) where you are going and when you expect to return. Take plenty of water, high-energy food supplies and protection against the sun, which can be very intense. The best practical guides to exploring Crete on foot are the two pocket books published by Sunflower Books called *Landscapes of Eastern Crete* and *Landscapes of Western Crete* (for maps see page 184).

Guided tours

If you want someone else to handle the logistics of getting to and from the start of your walk, consider joining one of the guided tours offered by The Happy Walker, Odós Tobazi 56, Réthimnon (tel: 0831 52920). This organisation offers a different walk each day of around 4-hours duration, led by a knowledgeable English-speaking guide.

When and where to go

Spring (from April to mid-May) is by far the best time to go walking on Crete because of the sheer wealth of wildflowers and the relatively cool but still pleasant weather.

Autumn (mid-September to October) also brings fine walking weather, but the countryside will be scorched by the summer heat, lacking spring's abundance of colour. The Samaria Gorge is Crete's most famous walk (see page 124) but as a result of its popularity, the path is crowded and noisy: for a quieter and equally magnificent route consider

Walking is the ideal way to experience the beauty of the Cretan countryside

walking the Ímbros Gorge instead (see page 140).

The south coast offers some excellent walking, using Loutró or Khóra Sfakíon as a base (see page 104). For more experienced climbers, the Levká Óri (White Mountains) present a serious challenge. The Kallergi mountain refuge (tel: 0821 54560), open from May to October, is run by the Greek Mountain Club (EOS), and is used by climbers as a base for crossing the range via Pákhnes (2,453m), Crete's second highest peak. Reaching the summit of Crete's highest mountain, Timíos Stavrós (a mere 3m higher at 2,456m), is relatively easy for fit and well-equipped climbers, by means of a path that leads up from the taverna alongside the Ídaean Cave (see page 100).

The Flowers of Crete

*V*isiting Crete in the summer, it is difficult to imagine just how colourful and rich in wildflowers this stony landscape can be in the spring. Geography and geology combine here to provide a myriad of different ecological niches. The climate varies from the frost-free coastal zone, via the temperate uplands to the alpine slopes of the central mountain ranges. Within these broad divisions, the range of soil types adds to the potential for diversity and a marked feature of Crete is the local abundance of some plants that are found in one site only, and nowhere else on the island.

When to go

The true wildflower enthusiast will find plants of interest throughout the year. The Cretan spring really begins as far back as October, when heavy rains bring the first crocus and narcissi bursting through the soil, and when the bare earth suddenly turns green almost overnight with new grass and freshly germinated seedlings. For sheer quantity of colour, however, the period from mid-April to mid-May is the main flowering season; this is the time when the slopes of the Levká Óri range turn from white to red as the snows melt and the scarlet anemones burst into flower.

Where to look

Almost every roadside offers a botanical feast in spring, but for rarer plants – especially orchids and bulbs – you need to head inland from the intensively cultivated coastal plains (where herbicides have, sadly, denuded the fields of their native flora) to the inland and upland regions. Almost any archaeological site will provide rich hunting ground for rare species because (with the exception of Knosós and Faistós) these sites are neither ploughed nor sprayed – hence exploring the archaeology of Crete becomes doubly pleasurable because of the wealth of colourful blooms. As an aid to identification *The Wildflowers of Crete*, an illustrated pocket guide written by George Sfikas, is inexpensive and widely available on the island.

What to look for

Rough uncultivated hillsides abound in various types of spurge, with their vivid lime-green flowers, and the thrusting 1m-high spikes of white asphodel. In unsprayed orchards and vineyards, purple oxalis competes with scarlet

Left: broom and aromatic herbs colour the scrubby hillsides in early summer
Below: Cretan bee orchid, pollinated by the insect it resembles

Left: Cretan ebony (*Ebenus cretica*), a species endemic to Crete

anemones. Easily mistaken for anemones, but with a lovely powdery sheen and a bell-shaped flower, is the Asiatic buttercup, *Ranunculus asiaticus*, often found on field edges and embankments. *Clematis cirrhosa*, with tiny yellow bellflowers, spotted inside, scrambles all over field walls, as do many pretty bindweeds. The white-flowered Cretan cyclamen blooms in shaded woodland and on damp banks. Among bulbs, irises, crocus, narcissi, lilies and alliums are relatively common, but the little species tulips and the plum-coloured fritilleries are far rarer. Purple and yellow-flowered orchids are easy to spot in grassland and on uncultivated slopes – though green, brown and white-flowered species take some finding amongst the mass of colour.

Wildflower sites

The following sites are especially rich in wildflowers. If you visit them, remember not to disturb the plants in any way, but leave them for future visitors and generations to enjoy.

Eastern Crete

Górtina (page 48) is renowned for flowers that seem to grow more luxuriously than elsewhere in this part of the island. Less visited are the flower-covered ruins of the Minoan village of Vasiliki on the western side of the road south from the National Highway to Ierápetra.

Western Crete

Two easily visited sites with abundant wildflowers are the German war cemetery at Máleme (page 108) and the ancient Minoan cemetery at Arméni (page 138). For a longer trip, Polirrínia (7km due south of Kastélli) is a marvellous spot for plant hunting. There is an excellent taverna in the modern village, right next to the beginning of the path that climbs up to the ancient hilltop city, or you can picnic in the ancient olive groves that surround the ruins. Meaning 'rich in lambs', Polirrínia was founded in the post-Palatial era (after 1100BC) and flourished until the Venetian era (13th

century), and its substantial remains shelter many kinds of bulbs and orchids.

The Vámos peninsula, especially around Litsárda and Selia, has many tiny fields surrounded by dry-stone walls where rock plants

Left: crown, or poppy anemone
Below: Asiatic buttercup

are abundant. The fields, where no longer cultivated, have been colonised by sheets of sky-blue lupins. Anópoli and Arádena, both accessible by road from Khóra Sfakíon (see page 104) combine an abundance of flowers, growing amongst cherry orchards and olive groves, with extensive coastal views.

DIRECTORY

'Drama is abundant in
the market.'
ADAM HOPKINS
CRETE

Shopping

Crete's four provincial capitals offer a huge range of choice, with scores of tiny hole-in-the-wall shops selling handmade leather goods, jewellery, textiles, ceramics and clothing, or village-made organic produce, such as honey, olive oil, dried herbs and nuts. Khaniá and Réthimnon are especially pleasant towns in which to shop, because of their characterful traffic-free back streets and large number of keen young artisans producing imaginative designs.

IRÁKLIO

Head straight for the market in Odós 1866 for the best choice in inexpensive souvenirs. Herbs, leather, Cretan-style leather boots, jewellery, embroidery, dried figs, sponges and loofahs are among the cornucopia of items on offer at good-value prices. If you like Cretan music, look out for the Music Market, on Odós 1821 (the street that runs parallel to the

market) or the nearby Record Shop, on the corner of Odós 1821 and Odós 1866, both selling tapes, CDs and videos. Also in Odós 1821 (at No 20) is Nick Papadogiannis, a more up-market shop dealing in objets d'art – Minoan-style and modern statuary, pottery and jewellery.

Odós Kalokairinou is Iráklio's principal shopping street – the place to go for clothes and everyday household goods. Odós 25 Augoústou contains a handful of interesting shops amongst the plethora of banks, car hire and travel agents: Eva Grimm (No 6) specialises in old Cretan handicrafts (antique woven cloth and wooden blocks for stamping biscuits, for example); Octopus (No 19) has a huge range of cheap clothes and inexpensive souvenirs and Minos Cretan Wines (No 12) needs no further explanation.

Fashionable, up-market clothing stores line the pedestrianised Odós Daidálos, and at the upper end, the side streets leading to the Archaeological Museum are dominated by shops selling fine reproductions of Cretan icons and Minoan jewellery and Cycladic sculpture: Galeria Dedalou (Odós Daidálos 11), Zeus Greek Art (Platía Eleftherías 3) and Elene Kectrinogianne (Platía Elefthérias 1) have the widest selections.

Sponges are among the bargains to be had in Iráklio's bustling market

If you are shopping for a picnic or a family meal, head for the covered markets

ÁYIOS NIKÓLAOS

Cheap souvenir shops dominate this resort, but better quality can be found in the two streets that run uphill from the harbour. Starting with Odós 28 Octóbriou, look for the shop on the right called Marieli which sells tapestries, handmade by the former journalist, Sofia Kana, using only natural dyes, plus modern jewellery, glass and ceramics. Chez Sonia, at No 20, is another outlet for antique Cretan costumes, and for more unusual contemporary crafts and

designs, including tapestries, puppets, ceramics and brasswork. On Odós Roussou Koundoúrou, Anna Karteri (No 7), has a better-than-usual selection of books, postcards and posters. Marisso (No 21) sells quality jewellery and, next door, Pegasus sells antique jewellery and modern jewellery incorporating ancient Greek coins. Round the next corner in Odós Sfakianaki, Maria Patsaki is an Aladdin's Cave of good things from antique embroidered Cretan blouses and waistcoats to old carpets and furniture.

Impromptu herb stall: Saturday is often the principal market day

cheap – made to last a lifetime, they will cost at least 20,000 drachmas.

Odós Khalídon

Cheap souvenirs account for most of the shops on this street, but do look out for colourful T-shirts, kaftans and beachwear at Nos 67 and 65. Opposite, Best is a browsing shop, full of colourful jewellery, painted wood toys and boxes, and woven straw hats. In the domed former Turkish bath on the right, you can watch a bronze-caster at work making scales, weights, bells, ornate candlesticks and door knockers. Further down, at No 5, Anatolita sells highly desirable ceramics and jewellery by the French artists, Juliette and Patrick Fabré.

To the Fortress

The narrow alleys of the old Venetian quarter leading up to Khaniá's fortress are dotted with shops selling the work of innovative young artists. Just as a sampler, walk up Odós Zambelioú and look for Bizarro, selling wacky waistcoats and blouses, plus exquisite puppets and dolls, Sokaki, selling jewellery made from glass beads, and Kamara, selling ethnic Cretan jewellery. Finally, on Odós Ageloú (running left from the entrance to the fortress) don't miss Top Hanao for the best selection of old Cretan rugs and tapestries you are likely to find on the island.

RÉTHIMNON

Slightly more expensive and perhaps a touch more up-market than Khaniá, Réthimnon is packed with shopping temptations. Leading up to the castle,

KHANIÁ

Khaniá market hall makes a good starting point for a shopping expedition, though you may get no further as you linger over stalls piled high with cheeses, herbs, honey, fish, fruit, meat and vegetables.

Leather Alley

Even more crowded and tempting is Odós Skridlóf, just down from the market, packed with stalls selling keenly priced leather bags, belts, sandals, wallets and shoes. Dig amongst the stalls and you will find one or two shops that don't sell leather: Tango (No 27) has some unusual jewellery and cast-glass lamps, No 31 sells videos and tapes of Cretan music and Mares, opposite, camping, walking, fishing and snorkelling gear. If you fancy a pair of handmade knee boots, Cretan-shepherd style, look for the boot and shoe shop at No 67, but don't expect these to come

Odós Salamínas has attracted young potters, painters and jewellers whose shops line both sides of the street. Below the castle, on Odós Katehaki, Zaharias Theodorakis has his workshop where you can watch him turning onyx by hand to make vases, bowls and lamps. Odós Arambatzoglou is packed with shops such as The Link, for ethnic jewellery, Talisman for hanging lamps and Dharma for hand-made clothes – just right for wearing to the disco. Also here is Olive Tree selling furniture, jewellery and hair ornaments of olive wood. In Odós Vernadou, which runs parallel, one block south, look for the Old Town Gallery, selling Judith Mooney's atmospheric watercolour paintings of Cretan village life.

Odós Ethníkos Anistáseos is the main shopping street for the townspeople, with a market at its upper end. For something truly local, look for Kogreion (No 41) selling worry beads in every imaginable colour and a ferocious array of knives. No 16 is a Dickensian antique shop where you may pick up an oil lamp amongst the miscellaneous junk. The little lane called Soulion has shops specialising in children's toys in painted wood and handmade dolls in Cretan costume.

Spoiled for choice: Khaniá's Leather Alley

Cretan Crafts

Some Cretan crafts – such as icon painting and jewellery making – have been revived in recent times by young, college-trained Cretans, keen to explore their ancient Minoan heritage. Their work is to be found in shops all over Crete and is remarkably good value, with jewellery, for example, selling at prices only a little above the cost of the raw materials. Other crafts, especially pottery and weaving, form part of a living tradition that has never died out, one that stems back 4,000 years to the Minoan era.

Pottery

Two villages specialise in the manufacture of pottery using timeless techniques. The potters of Margarítes, mid-way between Iráklio and Khaniá, supply many shops in Crete but you can buy more cheaply, and watch the pots being made, by seeking them out at their source. Vases, and pots intended as tableware are glazed a vivid azure blue – the same blue used for painting the house exteriors in this unspoiled village. You can also see a whole range of humbler stoneware and salt-glazed vessels – olive jars, bread-kneading troughs and jugs for olive oil or wine.

Ilias Ceramica, at the entrance to the town, has the widest selection of pottery shapes and colours. For giant terracotta *pithoi*, just like those found in Minoan palaces, head on up through the town and out to the other side to Ceramica Kallerges (on the right) and Nickos Kaugalakis (further up on the left).

The other village Thrapsanó lies to the southeast of Iráklio, near Mirtiá. Here the abundant red clay is simply scooped from the ground, shaped into giant *pithoi* and fired in wood kilns. Standing over 1m tall, they do not make ideal souvenirs for carrying home, but there are lots of smaller pots for sale in the numerous shops in the village and lining the Kastélli road.

Shoulder bags, Cretan style

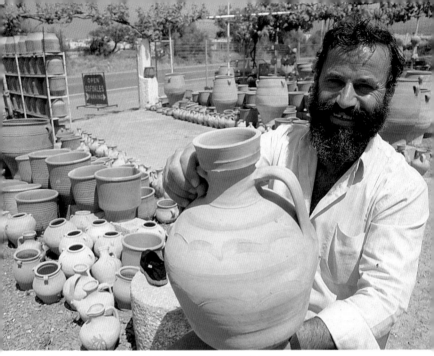

Buy direct from the producers for the best bargains in handmade pottery

Weaving

Antique woven cloth and tapestries, if you can track them down, are richly coloured from the use of vegetable dyes, and decorated with simple zig-zags, diamonds or stripes (good examples are displayed in the Museum of Cretan Ethnology in Vóri – see page 76). Woven from wool on a small horizontal loom, textile lengths are finished by knotting the warp threads and stitching lengths together to make bedspreads, knapsacks, saddle cloths, aprons, towels and tablecloths. Many towns in Crete sell woven bags and wall hangings, but to see the weavers at work it is best to go to Anóyia (not far east of the pottery town of Margarítes – see above) or to Kritsá, on the hill to the southwest of Áyios Nikólaos.

The house-fronts in both villages are hung from rooftop to pavement level with examples of weaving, and there is more inside. The loom is often situated just inside the front door of the shop, so that the black-clad women weavers can rush out and grab any potential customers, sometimes physically pushing and pulling them into the shop while keeping up a stream of sales patter in broken English or German.

Be prepared to be tough-skinned in seeking out precisely what you want and comparing prices before you buy. Do not pay over the odds for mass-produced rugs decorated with motifs from Minoan frescos, such as leaping dolphins, acrobats and bulls. On the other hand, do not expect genuine handmade textiles to come cheap. If you are easily intimidated by aggressive sales techniques, you may find it more enjoyable to go instead to Top Hanao (see page 152), the shop in Khaniá that specialises in genuine handwoven rugs and bedspreads.

Entertainment

Discos abound in Crete's towns and holiday resorts, patronised as much by local youth as by holidaymakers. You do not have to look far for the disco scene – neon lights and a throbbing beat will guide you, not to mention milling crowds in best party dress.

Other forms of entertainment are far harder to find on Crete, the choice often being limited to drama in the open-air theatres of Réthimnon or Iráklio (incomprehensible if you do not understand Greek) or rather saccharine performances of Cretan music and dance, usually provided as part of a carefully packaged 'Cretan Evening' and heavily promoted by tour agents.

Discos

Cretan discos are pretty relaxed by the standards that prevail in many European cities. Dress codes are unheard of, and there is often only a minimum admission fee – the disco makes its money from the sale of drinks but, this being Crete, the prices are not extortionate by any means. A popular activity is cruising from one disco to the next, looking for the best party atmosphere.

Cretan music

An evening spent listening to authentic Cretan songs, variously jolly and wistful, plaintive and rumbustious, can be a memorable experience (if you drink too much *raki*, as you will surely be encouraged to do, you may also end up with a very memorable headache!). The melody in Cretan music is usually played on the three-stringed lyra, which sounds like a violin, accompanied by the flute,

guitar, drum, bagpipes and the lute-like *bouzoúki*. Sometimes the vocalist and lyra throw the tune about, taking it in turns to weave ever more complex variations, with the other instruments providing a driving rhythm that sounds like an Irish jig gone Arabic. Many tavernas offer live music as a background while you eat, but for a taste of the real thing, head for the Café Crete, also known as the Lyrakia, at Odós Kalergon 22, Khaniá. This very basic hole-in-the-wall café behind the Arsenal is where Khaniá's traditional musicians gather for jam sessions and impromptu dancing. The atmosphere is warm and welcoming, especially on Friday night when hundreds of villagers descend on Khaniá for the next day's big street market.

Dancing

Khaniá is also one of the best places to watch traditional dancing from all over the Greek archipelago. The venue is the Firkás Theatre, the rather grand name given to the inner courtyard of the Old Venetian Fortress at the northwestern tip of the harbour. Performances, lasting two hours, take place at 9pm every Monday and Thursday, featuring 32 dances from different parts of Greece, each in appropriate costume. The admission ticket includes free *raki*.

Choose whether you want your dancing ancient or modern

Open-air cinema

Cretans are very fond of the cinema and open-air screenings are commonplace in summer in the outdoor theatres in the fortresses at Khaniá and Réthimnon, or in the lee of the city wall below the Archaeological Museum in Iráklio. Screenings are in the original language, with Greek subtitles. Cretan audiences are very noisy, so you may need to listen hard to hear the sound-track dialogue. Look out for fly posters advertising these, and more conventional indoor screenings.

Festivals

*E*aster is the big festival on Crete and many people come to the island just for this three-day period of religious and secular spectacle. Bear in mind, though, that the dates of Easter and most other religious festivals vary from year to year, not always co-inciding with the Orthodox calendar of the western church.

Easter rites

Good Friday (Epitafiós) is marked by solemn processions in which a shrouded bier, representing the dead Christ, is carried around the village to the accompaniment of prayers and mournful song. At midnight the following day, Easter Saturday, all lights are extinguished and the priest (traditionally using flints, but these days more prosaically using a cigarette lighter) produces the first flame of the new Christian year, symbolising resurrection and renewal. Members of the congregation light their candles from this flame, to the chant of *Khristós anésti* (Christ is Risen). This marks the end of the service, when church bells peal, firecrackers explode and, in some districts, bonfires are lit on which a dummy, representing Judas, the disciple who betrayed Christ, is burnt. Easter Sunday is then spent in feasting, traditionally on spit-roasted lamb.

Good Friday procession

Saints' days

Lamb features again on the Feast of Áyios Yeóryios (St George; this is celebrated on 23 April, or, if Orthodox Easter happens to be very late in the month, on the Monday and Tuesday after Easter Sunday). St George is very popular on Crete because, amongst his

Candle flames for the Resurrection (right) and a traditional Easter breakfast of red-dyed eggs

many other responsibilities, he is the patron of shepherds. Sheep and goat farmers take their flocks to church to be blessed, and one of their number is sacrificed to provide the traditional St George's Day dish of charcoal-grilled, herb-and-rice-stuffed lamb.

Every Cretan village also celebrates its own saint's day with a church service followed by singing, dancing, drinking and feasting. Visitors are warmly welcomed, so ask at the tourist office for details of any village name days coming up in the vicinity at the time of your visit. One that is certain to be celebrated all over the island, given that many churches are dedicated to the Panayia (the Virgin Mary) is August 15th, the Feast of the Assumption.

Wine and food

Amongst the best festivals for atmosphere are the wine festivals held in different parts of the island from early August to the end of October, an excuse for finishing off last year's wine and sampling this year's *raki*. More of an acquired taste is Khokhalithorradia (The Night of the Snails), celebrated by the mollusc-loving inhabitants of Vámos in April. Autumn brings the chestnut harvest in Élos, and with it an excuse to eat chestnut-flavoured sweets of all kinds, washed down with yet more *raki*, on the first Sunday after 20 October.

Arts festivals

Throughout the main holiday month of August, major towns mount one or two-week arts festivals; a feast of dancing, parades, music, theatre and exhibitions of paintings and crafts.

Children

*A*lmost nothing on Crete is geared specifically to children's tastes, and yet most children who come to the island on holiday succeed in having a marvellous time. In the process, however, their parents will probably end up being pestered to exhaustion by endless questions provoked by the magical strangeness of everything.

Cafés and tavernas warmly encourage families with children

When visiting Crete with children it is an advantage to choose a resort that has not been swamped by tourism, so that the everyday rhythms and activities of Cretan life can be allowed to take over. Many of the quieter resorts on the south coast – scarcely more than fishing villages – offer safe bathing, traffic-free streets and the chance to do and see things Cretan. Breakfast on creamy yoghurt flavoured with wildflower honey, shop at the local bakers for fresh bread and syrup-soaked pastries, watch fishermen clean their

catch mend their nets, marvel at the myriad of fish darting among the rock pools by the harbour, and say hello to the laden donkeys as they clip-clop mournfully up the street.

Archaeology and caves

To the horror of purists, most archaeological sites on Crete are completely unprotected from the erosive effects of visitors' feet and nobody seems to mind that hordes of visitors scramble over 4,000-year-old walls, staircases and courtyards. In fact, short of building a viewing platform above the site, it would be impossible to see the excavated remains without walking all over them. This presents a great opportunity for children who love exploring ruins and getting lost in the labyrinthine network of streets, corridors and storerooms making up a typical Minoan site. For added gloom, dankness and awesome rock formations, the Dhíktean Cave (see page 70) is a must.

Boat trips

The seas around Crete are normally as calm as a pond (though they get rough as autumn sets in, from mid-October, and can continue choppy well into April). Well worth considering are the boat excursions from Áyios Nikólaos or Eloúndha out to Spinalónga Island (see page 74), or the south-coast ferry service linking Palaiókhora, Soúyia and Ayía

Parks such as this are not common, but Crete is packed with magical adventures

Rouméli. For something a little less adventurous, but equally rewarding, go to Yeoryioúpoli (see page 126) and hire a pedal boat for exploring the Vrýsanos river, with its terrapins, crabs and rich bird life.

Food

Cretans love young children and there is no better way of ensuring indulgent service in tavernas than turning up with yours in tow. They are quite likely to be whisked off to the kitchens and introduced to all the members of the taverna owner's extended family. Despite the language barrier, you may find that your children have become firm friends with those of the taverna owner before too much time passes, guaranteeing that you and they are treated like old friends. Few tavernas serve special children's dishes but most menus feature pizza, pasta, omelettes, chicken and chips.

Tots in Crete

If you are travelling to Crete with very young children you can hire a range of equipment from an English-run firm called **Tots on Hols** (tel and fax: 01841 26276). Though based in Áyios Nikólaos, they will deliver everything from pushchairs and child car seats to cots, playpens and toys anywhere on the island. Advance booking is strongly recommended, especially in the high season (15 July to 15 September).

Sport and Beaches

*I*n the heat of a Cretean summer, few visitors to the island come with the objective of working out and limbering up. Crete caters more for the beach-loving sybarite than the fitness freak, and only recently have any kind of organised facilities been made available.

Water sports

For those who find sitting on the beach a touch monotonous, there are now two waterparks to choose from, both located in Khersónisos, to the east of Iráklio. Star Waterpark (tel: 0897 24434) is on Beach Road, near the Eri Hotel, and offers a huge range of activities, from waterslides and beach volleyball to jet skis, waterski-ing, windsurfing and para-sailing. Admission is free – you just pay for the activities that appeal to you. Aqua Splash (tel: 0897 24950) is located in countryside just to the north of Khersónisos on the Kastélli road. Here you pay an admission charge and then use all the facilities for free, including such attractions as the well-named Kamikaze water-slide.

Diving

The seas surrounding Crete are still relatively clean and teeming with fish, as anyone can tell just by looking into rock pools. Added to this, the sea floor is covered in antiquities, and because of this diving is very strictly controlled. Two organisations are licensed to train divers and take them on recreational trips to the seabed: one of them is the Atlantis Diving Centre based at the Grecotel, Adeloanos Kampos, Réthminon (tel: 0831 71002) and the other is the Paradise Dive Centre, at Odós Giamboudaki, also in Réthminon (tel: 094 333773). Both provide English-speaking trainers and guides and offer introductory dives of half-a-day or a day's duration or four-day courses

Natural (left) and man-made pleasures (above) are both on offer on Crete

leading to the internationally recognised PADI diving diploma.

Beaches and watersports

Calm waters and lack of wind do not make the ideal conditions for windsurfing, but equipment can be hired from local shops or from beachside huts in Almyrída (see page 126) and Khersónisos (near Mália). In Palaiókhora, the English-run Westwind Windsurfing School (located in a group of huts on the north end of the western beach) will supply boards, tuition and wetsuits, and they run their own rescue boat service.

Beach and watersport activities on Crete, in general, depend upon entrepreneurial young Cretans (sometimes Germans or English) setting up a makeshift stall on the beach for the season. The situation differs from year to year, but you are almost certain to find somebody offering the questionable pleasures of 'banana' rides, waterski-ing and paragliding if you head for the major resort beaches of Mália, Áyios Nikólaos, Áyios Paulos or the resort strip west of Khaniá.

Beach etiquette

Topless bathing is the norm on Cretan beaches, and nude bathing, although officially illegal, is commonplace in the less accessible coves and beaches of the south coast. If in doubt, take your cue from the behaviour of others on the beach. Once off the beach, however, you are expected to dress with decorum, and not upset local sensibilities by walking around in revealing beachwear.

Food and Drink

*E*verywhere you go in Crete, even in the remotest villages, you are sure to find a simple taverna serving inexpensive home-cooked food, open from breakfast time to late at night. Tavernas are ubiquitous, but do not expect any great variety amongst the dishes on offer: menus are virtually identical, from one end of the island to the other.

How, then, do you select a taverna, especially when faced with the plethora of choice that exists in the popular resorts and in the harbour areas of Khaniá and Réthminon? Start by ignoring any restaurant that employs touts to attract custom, and treat with suspicion any that display glossy pictures illustrating the dishes on offer. These tourist tavernas are, on the whole, more expensive and worse value than the simple unpretentious tavernas used by local people. If you want a hearty Greek salad that clearly hasn't been portion-controlled, or a generous-sized swordfish steak, instead of a piece the size of a postage stamp, avoid the tourist areas. Be prepared to sacrifice the harbour views in favour of better value and better cooking in the back streets and side alleys.

Menus
Restaurants in big towns will usually present a multi-lingual menu, but in village tavernas you may simply be taken to the kitchen and shown what is available. Menus will usually indicate whether fish is fresh or frozen. Most fresh fish is priced by the kilo and can be very expensive if you choose exotic varieties, such as lobster, but very good value if you stick to local fish. A red mullet or red snapper, for example, typically weighing 0.75kg, makes a substantial and inexpensive meal for two.

Booking
Nobody bothers to book tables in Crete (few tavernas have telephones anyway) and space will always be found for newcomers on the 'more the merrier' principle – in any event, there is always another almost identical taverna next door.

Prices
Just as menus vary little, so prices are consistent across the island. The price of the meat will vary according to what you eat rather than where, with fresh fish being more expensive than meat, and baked or stuffed dishes being cheapest of all. Some restaurants, especially those located in the provincial capitals, are trying to move up-market, offering a more formal ambience than the traditional taverna. These are slightly more expensive and are indicated in the text by a **$$** symbol (three-course meal for two with local wine costing around 7,500 drachmas) as opposed to the **$** symbol (the same for around 5,000 drachmas).

EASTERN CRETE

IRÁKLIO
For all its size, Iráklio does not have a huge choice of restaurants. For best value, head for Fotíou Theodosáki, the alley linking Odós 1866 and Odós Evans. The numerous and nameless tavernas

here are busy with market customers and traders during the day and serve authentic Cretan baked dishes and roast meats.

3/4 $$
Smart new restaurant on the old harbour serving international cuisine with fine views of the spotlit fortress.
Odós Theotokopoúlou 1.

Giovanni $$
Typically Cretan, set in a quiet back lane dripping with bougainvillaea, just off Odós Daidálou.
Odós Koraí 12.

Faros $$
Tipped by locals as the best in the city for fresh fish.
Odós Meteórou.

Loukoulos $$
Serves a good range of authentic pizzas, cooked in a wood-fired brick oven, plus Italian-style fish and vegetarian dishes.
Odós Koraí 5.

Minos $
Good value traditional Cretan cooking on the popular pedestrian shopping street.
Odós Daidálou 10.

New China $$
Set in an elegant town house in a quiet alley, authentic Cantonese food with a good choice of dishes featuring crab, squid or prawns (closed Sunday).
Odós Koraí 1.

Psaria $$
Situated at the harbour end of this busy street, some tables enjoy good views down over the fortress, but there is a lot of traffic noise. The salads and seafood can be excellent, but popularity has led to offhand service.
Odós 25 Augoústou.

Veneto $
Smart restaurant with a rooftop terrace and harbour views serving an adventurous mixture of Greek and Italian dishes. Try squid stuffed with rice, lemon, basil and pine nuts; aubergines baked with ham and cheese or any of the excellent salads.
Odós Epiménidou 9.

The prices are often the same, so choose a restaurant that offers the best view

Vizandio $

The pavement tables sheltered by (plastic) vines and (real) bougainvillaea spill round into pedestrianised Odós Daidálou. Serves everything from inexpensive pasta and pizza to veal dishes and grilled meats.
Odós Byzántiou.

ARKHÁNES
Grill Sabouda $

Clean and wholesome, serving cheap pasta dishes, stuffed vegetables and grilled meats.
On the junction, where the one-way traffic system begins.

Orestes $

A safe bet for authentic home-cooked Cretan food.
At the roundabout in the centre of the village.

ÁYIOS NIKÓLAOS

Tourist-trap restaurants line the harbour and the south side of Lake Voulisméni. As always, the more interesting restaurants are located a block or so back from the seafront.

New Kow Loon $$

Dishes such as squid in black bean sauce and steamed fish with ginger make a welcome change from Cretan fare.
1 Odós Pasifais (behind the tourist information centre).

Pelagos $$

Excellent fish tavern set in a neo-classical mansion, with a fishing boat beached in the front garden. Dine out of doors in the attractive rear garden. Good value *fruits de mers* (seafood salad).
Odós Koráka 9.

Zefiros $$
Lively spot serving all the typical Cretan dishes.
At the start of Aktí Koundoúrau (the seafood promenade).

ELOÚNDHA

Eloúndha's seafront is lined with restaurants all serving the same fish menus. The prices here, reflecting the cost of fresh seafood, tend to be higher than in many parts of Crete, but you can stick to pasta or omelette for a budget meal, or go to the big and boisterous Pizzeria $ on the north side of the harbour. The following are listed in the order that you encounter them, walking southwards from the harbour.

Vritomartes $$
Built on an artificial island in the harbour, less pricey than some, and selling more unusual types of fish caught by the restaurant's own boat.

Poulis $$
A typical Eloúndha restaurant offering mixed fish platter (portions of lobster, shrimps, red mullet, red snapper, squid, octopus, swordfish and sole).

Olandi $$
Offers a *meze* of six different starters and five main dishes – a chance to sample a wide range of Cretan food.

Be Be Que $$
Specialises in spit-roast meats.

Kalidon $$
Salmon crêpes and bouillabaisse are among the more usual items on the menu.

LASÍTHIOU PLAIN

TZERMIÁDHO
Kri-Kri $
Distinguishes itself from the other tavernas in town by serving freshly cooked food (not cooked earlier and warmed up) along with home-made wine served from the barrel.
On the main street.

ÁYIOS YEÓRYIOS
Roula Pepi $, Dias $ and Rea $
Opposite the war memorial, all serve local dishes (rabbit in season) and village wine, and make a good alternative to the more crowded restaurants of nearby Psikhró.

MÁLIA
Huge numbers of tavernas line the main street of this popular resort, most offering Cretan food tailored to British tastes. For something more authentic, head for nearby Mílatos, which has several very simple but good restaurants (the Agrogiala, Meraklis, Sirenes and Merry Helen, all $) serving fresh fish on the pebbly beach.

MÁTALA
The lovely beachfront is lined with west-facing tavernas, all with terraces designed to make the most of the views and the soothing sound of the breaking waves. There is little to choose between one taverna and the next: Panoramica, Alexis, Zorba's, and Maria's all specialise in fresh fish (all $), Sirlaki ($) offers wine from the barrel and charcoal-grilled meats and Waves ($$) specialises in lobster.

MIRTÍA
Kazantzákis $
Posters of alpine scenery (intended to make German visitors feel at home), decorate the walls of this taverna in the central square serving excellent local food.

PSIKHRÓ
Zeus $
Clean and efficient, serving typical
Cretan food, but can be busy with tour
buses.
Opposite the turning to the Dhíktean Cave.

IERÁPETRA
Just up from the Venetian Fortress, on
Odós Samóyha, is the Phesteria $ tavern,
which prides itself on fresh fish grilled
over charcoal. Further up the same
street, all with beachside tables, are the
Ouseri Manos, Kyknos, Konaki,
Castello, Napoleon and Sea Horse (all
$), serving an assortment of standard
taverna fare at, surprisingly, not
unreasonable prices.

SITIÁ
Paragadi $
Set amidst a run of seafront restaurants,
specialises in bouillabaisse, langoustine
and mullet.
Odós Karamáli.
Pizzeria da Giorgio $
Extensive pizza menu, with tables set
under the shade of a big pine tree.
Odós Dhimákratou.
Mixos $
Much liked by locals, with imperious and
unsmiling waiters (all part of the act)
serving excellent mixed grilled fish and
chicken, spit-roasted over a glowing
charcoal fire.Tables spill out onto the
street in summer.
Odós Kornarou 112.
Zorbas $
This huge taverna with tables on the
harbour and round two other sides of the
block, nevertheless offers snappy service.
Visitors come to enjoy huge plates of
mixed souvlaki or mixed grilled fishand
to enjoy the bustling atmosphere.
Odós Venizéou 64

WESTERN CRETE

KHANIÁ
Khaniá is the gourmet capital of Crete,
with scores of good tavernas lining the
long harbour front, and as many more in
the characterful alleys of the old city
beneath the fortress. The waterfront
restaurants divide roughly into three
sections. Nearest the fortress (on Aktí
Koundouriotis) are the young, noisy,
popular and reasonably cheap tavernas.
Beyond the Mosque of the Janissaries
(on Aktí Tombazi) are the quieter more
sophisticated (and more expensive)
establishments. Around and beyond the
Arsenal buildings (on Aktí Enoseos) come
the tavernas most favoured by local
people – more typically Cretan in the
informal and friendly management style
(and occasionally offering dishes you will
not find elsewhere, such as salads made
of wild leaves).

Alana $
Set in an old Venetian house with a
courtyard garden. Live Cretan music
nightly from 7.30pm.
Odós Zambeliu 19.
Aposteles $
Locally favoured taverna serving
unusually generous fish portions.
*Junction of Aktí Enoseos and Odós
Sarpidóna.*
Carnáyo $
Very popular with locals, with an
extensive menu that includes such exotica
as snails and sea urchins (or, as the menu
graphically calls them, 'sea hedgehogs').
*Platía Katehaki (the square beside the
Arsenal building and Customs House).*
Dinos $
Justifiably popular seafood taverna.
*At the far eastern end of the Venetian
harbour, on the corner with Odós Sarpidóna.*

Emerald Bistro $

For homesick or would-be Celts, a hospitable Irish-run restaurant serving draught Guinness, plus both Greek and Irish dishes.

Odós Kandiláki 17.

Golden Wok $

Good Chinese, also serving Thai and Korean dishes.

Aktí Tombazi (at the end nearest the mosque).

Good Heart $

Declares itself to be one of the `oldest and best Greek restaurants' in Khaniá. Whether this is true or not, it does offer live music every night, and serves a hearty octopus and olive stew.

Odós Kondiláki.

Kariatis $

Good value pizzeria and spaghetteria favoured by students at the local Technical University.

Behind the Customs House in Platia Katehaki.

Monastiri $$

Fine views of the lighthouse and fortress, live music nightly from 8.30pm and specialises in barbecued fish, chicken or steak.

Aktí Tombazi.

Oleander $

A good choice for those who have had their fill of *souvlaki* and swordfish: chicken kiev, beef stroganoff and veal escalopes stuffed with ham and cheese feature on the menu of this taverna, lined with dark wood panels and hung with stills from famous Hollywood movies of the 50s.

Odós Skufon (off Odós Zambeliu).

Semiramis $

Atmospheric place with a big garden for eating out of doors and live Cretan music 6.30–10.30pm nightly.

Odós Skufon (opposite Oleander, above).

Several restaurants in Khaniá have attractive patios or courtyard gardens

Suki Yaki $$

Despite a Japanese-sounding name, Suki Yaki is an up-market Chinese restaurant (also serving Thai dishes to add to the ethnic confusion) next to the Archaeology Museum.

Odós Hálidan.

Sultanas $

This colourful restaurant, hung with tapestries and carpets, occupies the former harem of a Turkish official and prides itself on home-style cooking.

Odós Moskon (next to the Ranieri Gate).

To Hani Garden Restaurant $

Specialises in more unusual Cretan dishes, such as *tsigariasto* (a Sfakiot goat-meat dish), *tourla* (lamb and cheese pie) and *dakos* (a salad of cheese, tomatoes and rusk). For parties of 12 who order 24 hours in advance, they will serve a Cretan Pilaf, a magnificent feast of rice and herb-stuffed mountain lamb. Live music nightly, 6pm to midnight.

Odós Kondiláki 26.

Réthimnon's waterfront cáfes look appealing, but better choices lie in the city centre

RÉTHIMNON

Avoid the multitude of overpriced restaurants lining the Aktí Venizélou beach road, and head for the Venetian harbour, where there is a good choice of seafood restaurants, or the alleys leading off Odós Arambatzoglou, where the pavement tables turn the whole area into one big outdoor party at night.

Cava d'Oro $

Perhaps the best of a run of seafood restaurants on the Venetian harbour. Standard fare here is 'Fisherman's Platter' – mixed grilled fish with mussels, shrimps and squid.
At the Custom House end of the Venetian Harbour.

Famagusta $

Try this Cypriot-owned restaurant if you are fed-up with the usual Cretan dishes. As well as Cypriot dishes (such as *sheftalia* – meat balls served with yoghurt), curries, stir-fried dishes and Japanese teriyaki are on the menu, and the special list of children's dishes features home-made fish fingers.
Platía Plastera 6 (west of the Venetian Harbour).

George's $$

One of the most popular tavernas in town, just up from the Rimóndi Fountain, its terrace sheltered from the sun by palm trees and vine-covered trellis. Special children's menu.
Odós Ethnikos Anistaseos.

Larenzou $

Characterful taverna with pavement tables beneath a pergola supporting a massive gourd plant.
Odós Zanthoudidou 29 (off Odós Arambatzoglou).

Minares $

Friendly taverna with a fine view of the Narantzies mosque and minaret.
Odós Vernadou.

Stelios Soumbasakis $

Simple taverna presided over by its jolly owner, serving home-made food, including vegetarian dishes.
In the square formed by the junction of Odós Arambatzoglou and Odós Nikiforou Foka.

Ziller's $$

Specialises in fillet steak in a number of different guises, but also does excellent grilled octopus and seafood dishes.
Platía Plastera 8.

VÁMOS PENINSULA

Demetros $
Fresh fish served on a terrace literally feet away from the sea, a romantic (and peaceful) spot at night.
Almyrída, north of Kalíves.

YEORYIÓUPOLI

Almiros $
The town's best restaurant, with an extensive range of good-value dishes.
On the south side of the main square.

Captain $
Charcoal-grilled dishes and *giros* (doner kebabs).
On the north side of the main square.

Poseidon $
Rough and ready taverna, reached down a 100-m long path, serving absolutely fresh fish caught by local fishermen.
On the right-hand side of the road leading out to the National Highway.

KOLIMVÁRI

Locals come to Kolimvári from all over Crete for seafood dishes. Try the Spatha ($$) taverna (on the eastern side of the main square), with its garden terrace and sea views, or the Diktina ($) and Argedina ($) tavernas, facing each other further north on the Moní Gonías road, beyond the post office.

PALAIÓKHORA

Many of Palaiókhora's restaurants are grouped round the central crossroad and the tables spill over the narrow pavements onto the road, causing havoc if any vehicle tries to get through.

Akropolis Ouzeri $

A thoroughly Cretan establishment, very plain and functional, serving local sausages and rabbit.
On the crossroad in the centre of the town.

Obelistherio $
Opposite the above and more geared to tourist tastes.

Caravella $
Specilises in freshly caught fish with tables right on the foreshore.
By the ferry harbour.

Christos $
Fresh fish or roast lamb.
Odós Venizélos, just before the tourist information centre.

Ostria $
Fresh fish and a lively atmosphere.
On the westernmost of Palaiókhora's two beaches.

Elite $
Worth seeking out on Saturday nights for its Cretan music and dancing.
At the far end of the western beach road, beyond the Hotel Elma

A light lunch costs remarkably little

The Cretan Menu

*T*he Cretan diet is the healthiest in the western world – and that's official. Medical studies into the Mediterranean diet were actually conducted on Crete, where it was found that people lived longer, were healthier in old age, and suffered from less heart disease and cancer than in other parts of Europe and the Americas. The principal components of this diet, until quite recently, were bread in very large quantities, accompanied by olives, lots of fresh fruit and raw vegetables, olive oil, red wine and protein in small quantities, principally in the form of goat's milk, cheese, walnuts or fish.

Tavernas

The legacy of this peasant diet can still be found on the menu of a typical Cretan taverna where you can eat heartily, and cheaply, on Greek salad (tomatoes, onions, cucumber, olives and *feta* – sheep's milk cheese), followed by fresh fish, or any number of healthily lean high-fibre dishes, such as stuffed vine leaves (*dolmadákia*), bean soup (*soupa fassólia*) or so-called field vegetables (*agria hórta*), a salad made of wild leaves, most of them related to the dandelion.

'Comfort food'

Fortunately Cretan tavernas also offer a lot of comforting food as well: spinach and cheese pies (*spanakopopita/ tiropitakia*) wrapped in filo pastry and oozing with flavour (and fat) for example, or macaroni and minced beef (*pastítsio*)

Tempting offers: seafood, stuffed vegetables or *souvlaki* (pork kebabs)

move on to a specialist pastry shop cum café, known as a *zakaroplasteion*. Here the cloying sweetness of the sticky pastries can be tempered by a strong Greek coffee (*métrio*, for medium sweet, *varí glikó* for sweet, *skéto* for without sugar), or a 'Nescafé' (the all-purpose term for all brands of instant coffee) served cold with a head of whipped milk, or hot with boiled milk.

Left: festive bread. Below: choose an *oúzo*

baked with a rich cheese sauce, or aubergine and minced lamb moussaka.

Grilled foods

Charcoal-grilled lamb, chicken, pork chops and steak are commonplace, but *souvlaki* remains the all-time favourite taverna dish, usually consisting of a barbecued pork kebab, though these days you will also find beef, lamb, mixed meats and fish *souvlaki* on most menus. Country tavernas may offer rustic dishes, such as casserole of rabbit (*kounéli*), pigeon (*pitsounia*) or wild boar (*agrióhiros*), whilst every beachside restaurant worthy of its name will offer a tempting choice of grilled fresh fish, such as bream, bass, mullet, snapper, swordfish and (usually imported) lobster.

Sticky desserts

Tavernas do not, as a rule, serve desserts, though most will provide a bowl of delicious yoghurt with honey if asked, or a selection of fruit. For *baklavás* (filo pastry stuffed with spiced almonds) or *kataifa* (shredded pastry filled with walnuts and syrup) it is traditional to

Alcohol

Retsina – white wine flavoured with pine resin – is an excellent accompaniment to Cretan food, but it is not a traditional Cretan wine. Some rural restaurants serve their own delicious home-made wine, drawing it directly from huge wooden barrels. Bottled local wines include Cava d'Or, Olympias, Gorthys, Tsantalia and Calliga, all of which are available in red, white or rosé versions. Cretan wine makers distil delicious *raki*, a clear brandy-like liquor, from the grape pips and skins left over from the wine making process. An *ouzeri*, similar to a traditional café (*kafenion*), serves the aniseed-flavoured aperitif known as *oúzo*, usually with little dishes of olives, fried potatoes or beans as an accompaniment.

Accommodation

*C*rete offers a huge range of accommodation, from simple 'rent rooms' in someone's home to luxurious self-contained resorts with private beaches, shops, restaurants and sports facilities. Most middle-range accommodation is located in small hotel or villa complexes where you can expect a simply furnished room with en-suite shower and toilet, a balcony for enjoying the sun and sometimes a small kitchen for preparing light meals.

Hotels

Hotels are classified into six categories (luxury, A, B, C, D and E) according to the standard of facilities and services on offer. Unless you want to live in the lap of luxury, A and B class hotels are adequate and comfortable for most visitors. Room prices are fixed according to the hotel's classification, but hoteliers will often (quite legitimately) get round this by charging for a whole range of extras, especially during the high season. You may find, for example that the hotel charges you extra if you only stay one night; it can also insist on charging you for breakfast, or even for half board

(breakfast and either lunch or dinner) even if you do not want to eat in the hotel. C class hotels do not usually have restaurants and so cannot do this. Some will levy a charge for supplying a television in your room or present you with a bill for electricity consumed by central heating or air-conditioning systems, so make sure you know what the likely cost is to be in advance.

Villas and self-catering

Many package-tour companies offer accommodation in villa complexes rather than hotels, and these are not subject to the same degree of government control, so you cannot always be sure of the facilities on offer. A key point to check before you book is the availability of heating and air-conditioning. Many villas have no heating, and this can result in a miserable holiday spent searching for warmth if, as can happen in April and October, cold wet weather sets in. Conversely, you may be glad of something more than an open window for keeping cool during the intense heat of a Cretan summer.

Rent Rooms

Private accommodation, known universally on Crete as 'Rent Rooms', can be had in every tiny village. Traditionally, the family rented out

The cheapest hotels may be above a busy restaurant: back streets could be quieter

spare rooms in their homes, but today's rent rooms are more likely to be in purpose-built blocks, equipped with kitchens and showers. Prices vary greatly, so you should shop around. It is accepted that you will want to see your room before agreeing to take it, and bargaining over the price is normal practice during the less busy seasons. Best discounts are given to people who intend to stay three days or more, and some owners will not rent rooms for a stay of only one night.

Go as you please

Most visitors to Crete base themselves in one place for a week or more, and travellers touring the island, staying at a different place each day, are still something of an oddity. Touring during the high season (July, August and early September) is made more difficult by the fact that most accommodation is pre-booked by tour operators. Touring in the spring and autumn is perfectly feasible, however, and you can sometimes secure big discounts on room rates from hoteliers keen for your custom.

Oddities

Cretan plumbing is far from efficient, so expect quirky showers and (except in the very classiest of hotels) do not put used toilet paper down the lavatory – put it in the bags or bins that are especially provided for this purpose. Annoyingly, Cretan chambermaids are employed to unmake your bed, rather than make it, so expect to have to remake your own bed every day.

On Business

*D*espite the warmth and genuine friendliness of Cretan hospitality, Crete remains a closed society, almost impossible for non-Cretans to penetrate when it comes to business. Almost invariably, those foreigners who have succeeded in establishing businesses in Crete have done so by marrying a Cretan and 'going native'.

Crete has only very recently emerged from the pre-industrial age, and though flashy types in BMWs are common enough in the provincial capitals, rural Crete still has a peasant economy, based on self-sufficiency and barter, rather than monetary exchange.

Tourist-fuelled growth

All this is changing because of tourism, which has brought rich, free-spending visitors to the island in ever-increasing numbers since the 1970s. The chief beneficiaries have been the owners of land or property in the coastal regions, where the landscape has been transformed by almost uncontrolled, and often speculative, hotel building. Being self-sufficient in many important resources, including building materials, Crete has rapidly developed its tourist infrastructure without building up huge trade deficits – in fact it imports very little (except for fuel, vehicles and industrial metals).

Agriculture

In return Crete has a healthy export trade, exploiting its abundant sunshine and fertile soils to grow citrus fruits, bananas, peppers, tomatoes, aubergines and cucumbers, gaining a premium price for these products in winter, when out of season salad crops are scarce.

Business opportunities in Crete are not yet very developed, but banks will help steer you through the maze

This view of the Mesarás plain awash with greenhouses is coming to typify much of Crete's landscape

Environmental issues

The income from intensive horticulture is slowly bringing benefits to the once-isolated southern coast of Crete, though not without controversy. As visitors to the major archaeological sites at Faistós and Górtina will discover, vast areas of the southern coastal plain are disappearing beneath a sea of plastic, as more and more farmers build polythene greenhouses to protect and warm their crops. Worse still, from an environmental point of view, unscrupulous landowners have deliberately set off major forest fires on the south of the island. Angered by plans to create a national nature reserve on potentially profitable land, they have destroyed the natural vegetation and left a virtual wilderness which will, no doubt, soon be planted with neat rows of saplings and glinting plastic tunnels.

Towards integration

In theory, Crete should become increasingly more open to foreign investment and overseas business involvement, now that, as part of Greece, it is a member of the European Union. Overseas banks have in fact started to open branches in Iráklio, the capital, in anticipation of this, and anyone planning to do business in Crete would do well to contact these banks for assistance.

As for Crete as a conference venue, the first tentative steps were taken in 1991 when the then Prime Minister of Greece, Constantine Mitsotakis, laid the foundation plaque of a new conference centre (combined with a Battle of Crete memorial chapel) at Galatás, just west of Khaniá, though subsequent progress has proved very slow.

Practical Guide

CONTENTS

Crete in the off-peak season (ie avoiding school holidays). Scheduled flights into Crete are expensive and involve a change of plane and terminal at Athens' airport. Alternatively, consider arriving in Crete the traditional way – by ferry from Piréas (the port of Athens).

Visas:

US, Commonwealth and European Union nationals can stay in Crete for up to three months without a visa. Officially, if you want to stay longer, you should apply to the tourist police for a visa, providing evidence that you can support yourself. Few people bother, since the checks on leaving Crete are minimal – even if you are fined for overstaying, the amount of money involved is negligible.

Airport facilities

Crete has two international airports – at Iráklio and Khaniá – serving the east and west of the island respectively. Often the tour operator dictates which airport you use, but if you have the choice, Iráklio is preferable, being a more modern airport (rebuilt in 1995), and relatively efficient. Delays at Khaniá are common and a tedious wait is made worse by the lack of facilities. Bear in mind that the travelling time between the two airports, using the fast National Highway, is about 2 hours and make your decision accordingly.

ARRIVING

Scores of tour operators sell package tours to Crete and this is by far the cheapest way of getting to the island. Flight-only deals on charter flights are available if you are prepared to visit

Onward travel

Tour operators meet their customers at the airport and arrange onward travel by coach or taxi. If you are on your own, you can also take a taxi – the fares from the airport to the main destinations around the island are fixed, but it would be wise to double-check and agree the fare in advance to avoid arguments at the other end.

Arriving by sea
Seperate ferries ply daily across the Sea of Crete between the ports of Piréas and Iráklio, Khaniá and Réthimnon. The journey takes around 12 hours and this is a remarkably cheap way to bring your car across, if you are touring Greece. Travel agents in any Greek city will handle bookings – be sure to get the direct sailings, rather than those that stop at various islands, unless you want to double the journey time.

CAMPING
Crete has some 20 or so official camping sites, graded A (luxury) to C (basic), and a complete list can be obtained from tourist offices in Crete. You need not limit yourself to these, however, because

although camping in the wild is against the law in Greece, plenty of enterprising farmers and landowners have put up 'Camping' signs on their land (especially on the roads leading to the popular beaches). In return for a small fee they will supply water and use of a kitchen, toilet and shower.

CHILDREN
Children are universally adored in Crete and taking yours on holiday will guarantee that you make lots of friends. On the other hand, Cretan children are treated as mini-adults, expected to eat the same food and stay up as late as grown-ups. Children's menus in tavernas are not common, but there is usually something they will readily eat (see also page 160).

CLIMATE
Crete is very hot and dry at the time of year when most people visit – from June to September – and the sun is intense. Cretans, wisely, stay indoors for the hottest part of the day and cover up when they go out, to prevent sunburn. Spring (April and May) is delightful by contrast, with flower-filled meadows and sunshine that is warm but not searing. Autumn begins in October and is marked by occasional prolonged downpours that can last a day or an hour, interspersed by days of brilliant blue skies and sunshine. Visiting Crete at this time of year can be a gamble because of the rain, but the island is becoming more popular as a winter-holiday destination, where it is possible to ski in the mountains during the day and eat out of doors by the coast in the evening – in winter the temperature by the sea rarely drops below 8°C and is often considerably warmer.

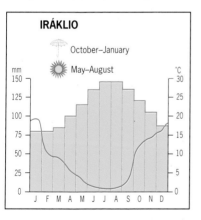

IRÁKLIO

October–January

May–August

mm — 150, 125, 100, 75, 50, 25, 0

°C — 30, 25, 20, 15, 10, 5, 0

J F M A M J J A S O N D

WEATHER CONVERSION CHART
25.4mm= 1 inch
°F=1.8x°C+32

Conversion Table

FROM	TO	MULTIPLY BY
Inches	Centimetres	2.54
Feet	Metres	0.3048
Yards	Metres	0.9144
Miles	Kilometres	1.6090
Acres	Hectares	0.4047
Gallons	Litres	4.5460
Ounces	Grams	28.35
Pounds	Grams	453.6
Pounds	Kilograms	0.4536
Tons	Tonnes	1.0160

To convert back, for example from centimetres to inches, divide by the number in the third column.

Men's Suits

UK		36	38	40	42	44	46	48
Rest of Europe	46	48	50	52	54	56	58
US		36	38	40	42	44	46	48

Dress Sizes

UK		8	10	12	14	16	18
France		36	38	40	42	44	46
Italy		38	40	42	44	46	48
Rest of Europe		34	36	38	40	42	44
US		6	8	10	12	14	16

Men's Shirts

UK	14	14.5	15	15.5	16	16.5	17
Rest of Europe	36	37	38	39/40	41	42	43
US	14	14.5	15	15.5	16	16.5	17

Men's Shoes

UK	7	7.5	8.5	9.5	10.5	11
Rest of Europe	41	42	43	44	45	46
US	8	8.5	9.5	10.5	11.5	12

Women's Shoes

UK	4.5	5	5.5	6	6.5	7
Rest of Europe	38	38	39	39	40	41
US	6	6.5	7	7.5	8	8.5

CRIME

Blissfully, Crete is relatively crime-free and the only anti-social behaviour you are likely to encounter is from other visitors. Even here, the lager louts stick to their own haunts and if you avoid late-night bars you are not likely to be troubled by their hooligan behaviour. Despite the lack of crime, do not be complacent – look after your valuables and do not leave them where a thief might be tempted.

CUSTOMS

There are no customs restrictions on the import and export of duty-paid purchases between Crete and other parts of the European Union. Limits do apply, however, on duty-free goods (those on which VAT has not been paid) imported from another EU country, and on goods from non-EU countries. The limits are as follows:

Duty-free EU/Non EU
Cigarettes 800/200
Cigars 200/50
Tobacco 1,000/250gms
Spirits 20/2 litres
Wine 90/2 litres

These are the amounts that can be imported into Crete. Some countries, including the USA, have far stricter limits on what may be imported from Crete.

CYCLING

Crete is becoming increasingly popular among the mountain-bike fraternity, with plenty of testing dirt roads, as well as rock-paved droveways to explore. Most cyclists bring their own bikes, because bike hire is by no means as common as motorbike or car hire, though there are plenty of shops in the main towns selling spares and accessories.

DRIVING

Cretans like to boast about their daredevil driving skills but in reality it is only the taxi drivers and a few flash drivers of expensive cars that behave badly on the roads of Crete. Most people stick to a sedate speed (forced to do so by the steep, twisting terrain) except on the main east–west National Highway, where the official speed limit (90kph) is often broken.

The National Highway is the island's main artery, running east–west across the top of the island. It is a good wide road, but, despite appearances, it is not a dual carriageway. The right-hand lane is only used if you want to pull over to let a faster car past – it combines the functions of a crawler lane and hard shoulder. It is not a continuous carriageway, and disappears altogether from time to time. You may also find vehicles, flocks of sheep and roadside stalls blocking this lane.

The island's other roads all feed into the National Highway, running north or – more often – south from it. These roads vary in quality from fast wide metalled roads with few bends to dirt tracks with massive potholes. In general, they are steep and twisting and when planning a journey you should estimate conservatively to average 25kph at the most.

During the rainy season (late October

to early April), expect rock falls and landslides to hamper your progress and be very wary of driving at speed over rough roads – it is easy to damage the rim of your wheels and end up with a flat tyre. Where there is only room for one car to pass, the Cretans tend to be aggressive; it is wise to let Cretans go first, but do not flash your lights to indicate that you are giving way – on Crete, flashed lights mean 'get out of the way, I'm coming through!'

Practicalities

There are almost as many car rental agencies on Crete as there are restaurants and bars (see page 21), so shop around for the best all-in-deal – that is, one that includes comprehensive insurance, collision damage waiver, and no mileage charges.

Drive on the right, wear seat belts in front and rear seats and observe the speed limits: 50kph (31mph) in town, 90kph (56mph) on ordinary roads and 90kph (56mph) on the National Highway. Drink driving is severely penalised. Petrol stations are ubiquitous and open long hours. Road signs are in English and Greek.

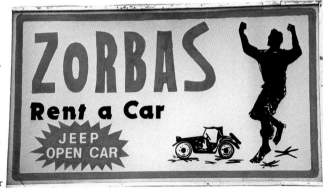

ELECTRICITY

Standard two-pin continental-type plugs are used on Crete and the supply is 220 volts/50 cycles. Visitors from the UK and USA/Canada need an adaptor.

EMBASSIES

There is a British consulate at Papalexándrou 16, Iráklio (tel: 081 224012), but all the other embassies are in Athens. If you need help, go to the tourist police in the first instance (see *Police* on page 186).

EMERGENCY TELEPHONE NUMBERS

Police 100
Ambulance 166
Tourist police 174
ELPA (Road Assistance) 104

HEALTH

The greatest hazards to health on Crete are the sun, sea creatures and mosquitoes. The sun is very intense and

it is very easy to burn, even just walking around, and even in the relatively mild spring weather, especially if you are exploring archaeological sites on exposed hillsides – wear a hat to protect your head and neck, and cover your arms. Jellyfish can give you a nasty nettle-like sting which takes up to a week to go down. There is no cure but patience and time, though the ammonia in urine is said to have a mildly relieving effect. Sea urchin spines are a greater hazard – these black creatures inhabit rocky shorelines and are nearly invisible against the rock, so always wear shoes or sandals when exploring rock pools. Spines can be extracted, like splinters, using a needle, but seek medical help if they go deep – they will quickly go septic if not removed.

Probably the most effective mosquito deterrents are the plug-in electrical devices which are widely available on Crete. The green pyrethrum insect repellent coils (*spíres* in Greek) are also fairly effective, but by no means foolproof, so take insect-bite cream.

Basic emergency care is free on Crete and there are good health clinics providing outpatient services from 8am to noon in every large town. These are signposted (with a red cross), so that they are not difficult to find.

LANGUAGE

Cretans are great anglophiles, and they watch English and American television programmes, so almost everyone speaks basic English. Even so the ability to read Greek characters will enrich your visit in many ways. Take care to get the stress right: every Greek word has an accent (´) over the syllable to be stressed and if you get it wrong, you are not likely to be understood.

It is helpful to know the Greek alphabet so that you can recognise placenames, while the few words and phrases following the alphabet will also come in handy.

Alphabet

Alpha	short *a*, as in hat	Iota	short *i* sound,	Taf	*t* sound
Beta	*v* sound		as in hit	Ipsilon	long *e*, as
Gamma	*y* sound, as in you	Kappa	*k* sound		in feet
Delta	*th* sound, as in	Lambda	*l* sound	Phi	*f* sound
	father	Mu	*m* sound	Chi	guttural *ch*
Epsilon	short *e*	Nu	*n* sound		sound, as in
Zita	*z* sound	Omicron	*o*		lock
Eta	long *e*, as in feet	Pi	*p* sound	Psi	*ps*, as in
Theta	hard *th* sound, as	Rho	*r* sound		lamps
	in think	Sigma	*s* sound	Omega	*o*

Basic vocabulary

good morning	*kaliméra*
good evening	*kalispéra*
goodnight	*kalinikhta*
hello	*yásou*
thank you	*efkharisto*
please/you're welcome	*parakaló*
yes	*ne*
no	*óchi*
where is...?	*pou ine?*
how much is...?	*póso káni?*
do you speak English?	*milate angliká?*
I don't speak Greek	*dhen milo ellinika*

Food and drink

food	*fagito*
bread	*psomi*
water	*nero*
wine	*krasi*
beer	*bira*
coffee	*kafes*
lobster	*astakos*
squid	*kalamares*
otopus	*oktapodhi*
red mullet	*barbounia*
whitebait	*maridhes*
lamb	*arni*
chicken	*kotopoulo*
meat balls	*keftedhes*
skewered meat	*souvlakia*
pork	*chirini*
spinach	*spanaki*
courgette	*kolokithia*
beans	*fasoles*
chips	*patates tiganites*
cucumber	*angouri*
tomato	*tomata*
olives	*elies*
salad with feta	*horiatiki*
tomato salad	*salata*
yoghurt and cucumber dip	*tsatsiki*

Numbers

1	*éna*
2	*dhío*
3	*tria*
4	*téssera*
5	*pénde*
6	*éxi*
7	*evtá*
8	*okhtó*
9	*enea*
10	*dheka*

Places

street	*odós*
square	*platia*
avenue	*leoforos*
room	*dhomatio*
post office	*tachidhromio*
police	*astinomia*
pharmacy	*farmakio*
doctor	*iatros*
bank	*trapeza*
café	*kafenion*

LOST PROPERTY

Cretans are instinctively honest and helpful and will turn in anything they find that they recognise to be important or valuable. Go to the tourist police if all else fails.

MAPS

The best general map of Crete currently available is the *Bartholomew Crete Holiday Map*. For walking, it is best to use the excellent Harms Verlag 1:80,000 series maps, which show every footpath. There are five sheets in the series and they are not widely available on Crete, so it is best to order them before you go from a specialist map shop.

MEDIA

All your favourite newspapers (and many magazines) are sold on Crete, the day after publication. Cretan TV broadcasts many films and programmes in English (with Greek subtitles) and one channel is devoted to US news.

MONEY AND TAX

Money-changers are ubiquitous, and some operate round the clock in the big resorts. All money changers (including the banks) advertise tempting exchange rates but hide the fact that they typically charge a 3 per cent commission on the transaction – for cashing Eurocheques and traveller's cheques as well as exchanging banknotes.

Shop around to see who offers the best combination of exchange rate and commission. Banks in big cities have hole-in-the-wall exchange machines, (ATMs) that will give you a cash advance using your credit card. These machines are temperamental, however, and occasionally swallow your money or card without giving anything in return. If this happens, go to the bank when it reopens, taking your passport as proof of identity. You should be able to retrieve your card at once, though getting your cash back may take longer.

As in all European Union countries,

Venetian-era map of Iráklio's harbour, in the city's Historical Museum

visitors from outside the EU can reclaim the Value Added Tax (which can be as much as 20 per cent) on high-value purchases – ask about the Tax Free Shopping scheme.

NATIONAL HOLIDAYS

Offices, banks and some shops close on national holidays, though in tourist resorts, it is business as usual as long as there is money to be made. The dates of Lent, Easter and other religious holidays in the Orthodox calendar vary from year to year and can be up to two weeks later in the year than the equivalent feasts in the western church calendar.

New Year's Day 1 January
Epiphany 6 January
Clean Monday Variable – two days before Ash Wednesday
Independence Day 25 March
Good Friday Variable
Easter Monday Variable
Labour Day 1 May
Ascension Day Variable
Whit Monday Variable
Assumption Day 15 August
Okhi ('No') Day 28 October
Christmas 25 December
St Stephen 26 December

OPENING HOURS

Museums Typically, the major museums and archaeological sites are open 8am to 3pm, with limited opening hours in winter, on Sundays and on public holidays. Admission is free on Sundays. Most close on Monday – Knosós and Faistós being among the chief exceptions.

Shops Stores catering to tourists open very long hours – typically from 10am to 10pm, or later. Street kiosks – selling everything from fruit and cold drinks to aspirins and razor blades – stay open even longer – some city kiosks literally never close. Shops and markets catering to the local population open 8am to 1.30pm Monday to Saturday, and 5.30pm to 8.30pm on Tuesday, Thursday and Friday only.

Monasteries and churches Though monasteries close from 1pm to 3pm, heavily visited ones may only close for an hour. If churches are locked it is polite to respect the privacy of the keyholder during the siesta hours of 1pm to 5pm.

Yes, it is a post office: in Crete they are found in yellow caravans or the main city square

Banks Typical hours are 8am to 2pm, Monday to Thursday and 8am to 1.30pm on Friday, but those in major resorts will open until later in the day.

Post offices Typical hours are 8am to 8pm, Monday to Saturday.

PHARMACIES
In Greek towns, the ØAPMAKAION (Farmakeion) serves the role of doctor and dispensary – the trained pharmacists who staff them can diagnose most common complaints and recommend a remedy. Though they observe the same opening times as local shops, there will always be one open on a late-night rota, details of which are posted on pharmacy doors or windows.

PLACES OF WORSHIP
Orthodox churches are a prominent feature of every town and village – with luck you will be able to witness a wedding, or a naming ceremony (similar to christening); these usually take place on a Saturday and Sunday, respectively. There are no Protestant, Jewish or Islamic places of worship on Crete, but there are Roman Catholic churches in Iráklio (on Odós Patros Antoniou) and in Khaniá (opposite the Archaeological Museum).

POLICE
Crete's tourist police are specifically trained to deal with common visitor problems and most speak English fluently. Many of the complaints they handle (such as cases of overcharging in restaurants and hotels) involve misunderstandings, rather than deliberate fraud, so they are principally there as diplomats to smooth ruffled feathers, but they will also swing into a sympathetic action if you are lost, stranded or just plain confused. Dial 174 from anywhere and ask for information and help, or you can go to a specific tourist police station, as follows:

Iráklio: on Odós Dhikeosínis 10
Réthimnon: on Prokimeá Venizélou (ie on the beachside road) in the same building as the tourist information office
Khaniá: on Odós Kareskáki

Regular police are more unpredictable. Much of the time, they ignore activities that are strictly against the law (parking in prohibited areas, nude or topless bathing, camping rough, breaking the speed limit). Occasionally, however, someone orders a clamp down, so be wary and avoid drawing attention to yourself by behaving in a conspicuous or insensitive manner. Be polite if you are approached by a policeman and usually you will be let off with a warning.

POST

You can buy stamps from kiosks and shops, but they make a small surcharge which you can avoid by going to a yellow post office caravan – these are to be found on the main square of major towns and are open 7.30am to 2pm (8pm in tourist areas) daily, with reduced hours on Sunday. In Iráklio, the caravan is on the western side of Platía Venizélou, by the entrance to the El Greco Park. In Khaniá it is on the cathedral square, off Odós Hálidhon.

PUBLIC TRANSPORT

Crete is covered by a comprehensive bus network with half-hourly services on the busy routes between the four provincial capitals, and four or five services a day on routes covering the remoter parts of the island. Timetables are available at the tourist information offices and at the bus stations in the four main cities, all of which are centrally located. Tickets are purchased in advance from kiosks at the bus termini, but are sold on board the bus if you join at a stop en route. Prices are very reasonable, and the buses are clean and comfortable, so, with a little forward planning, this can be a good way of touring Crete.

Taxis

Taxis are used for long-distance journeys, as well as short trips across town. There are fixed fares for some journeys but you should always check and agree the fare in advance to avoid misunderstanding. You can also hire taxis by the day or half day for sightseeing, and you can book taxis to drop you and return to collect you later in the day – for example, at the beginning and end of the Samaria Gorge walk.

There are places on Crete where a car can't go

Coaches

Signing up for one of the ubiquitous coach excursions offered by travel agents in every Cretan town is another way of getting to the most popular destinations – the main advantage being that the logistics are all handled for you.

SENIOR CITIZENS

There are no reduced-price concessions for senior citizens on Crete. On the other hand, not being tied to school holidays, senior citizens can visit Crete at the quietest and cheapest times of the year. Room rates are lowest in April, May and October and, if you choose to overwinter in Crete, self-catering accommodation can be found for as little as £5 a day.

STUDENT AND YOUTH TRAVEL

Holders of international student identity cards qualify for reduced-price admission to most museums. Crete is, in many respects, a cheap destination, and very popular with young people as a result. Some come to Crete for the whole season, doing casual work in bars, tavernas or shops. The pay is poor, or non-existent, but you may be given free accommodation, paid a commission or allowed to keep the tips.

TELEPHONES

Card-operated and coin-operated payphones for local calls and international calls are everywhere in Crete – in shops, cafés, hotels and street booths. You can also use the phone at the ubiquitous street-side kiosks that sell newspapers and sundries. Here the calls are metered and the kiosk attendant will tell you the cost at the end (adding their own mark up).

For long-distance calls it is cheapest to go to one of the OTE offices that are found in nearly every town (opening hours vary from round-the-clock in Iráklio and Khaniá, to 6am to midnight in major resorts, to 7.30am to as early as 3pm elsewhere). Calls are metered and paid for at the end.

For calls outside Greece, dial 00 first, followed by the country code (Australia: 61, Eire: 353, New Zealand: 64, UK: 44, USA and Canada: 1). For reverse charge/collect calls, dial the international operator on 161. You may find it difficult to place an international call at peak times.

TIME

Crete is 3 hours ahead of GMT in summer, 2 hours ahead in winter.

TIPPING

Tips are expected on Crete (in some cases, this is the only source of income for the waiters and bar staff), so round up the figures to the nearest whole number or leave the small change in cafés and tavernas. Taxi drivers expect around 10 per cent, and a small tip should be placed in the toilet attendants' dish before using public facilities. It is also customary to tip tour guides and to give a small donation to priests if they open up the church for you and give you a tour.

TOILETS

Public toilets are available in most towns, but often hidden somewhere easy to overlook, so most people use café toilets (which are much better) – having first ordered a drink. Toilet and shower blocks are found at most of the popular beaches, but their cleanliness varies. Remember, too, that toilet tissues should never be placed down the toilet, but put into the wastepaper basket

Camping in the wild is against the law but typically Cretans turn a blind eye

provided. Failure to do this is usually the reason why Cretan toilet facilities get blocked, with floors awash with unpleasant deposits.

TOURIST INFORMATION
Branches of the official Greek National Tourist Organisations (EOT) can be found in the provincial capitals, as follows:

Iráklio: Odós Xanthoudídou 1 (opposite the entrance to the Archaeology Museum), tel: 081 228203/228225.

Khaniá: Odós Kriári 40 (Pantheon Building), tel: 0821 26426.

Réthimnon: Prikiméa E Venizélou (the waterfront promenade), tel: 0831 29148/24143.

Áyios Nikólaos: Aktí I Koundorou 20 (facing on to Voulisméni Lake), tel: 0841 22357.

Overseas offices of the Greek National Tourist Office are in:
UK: 4 Conduit Street, London W1R 0DJ (tel: 0171 734 5997).

USA: 645 Fifth Avenue, Olympic Tower, New York, NY 10022 (tel: 212 421 5777).plus in Chicago and LA

Australia: 51–7 Pitt Street, Sydney, NSW 2000 (tel: 2 241 1663).

Canada: 1300 Bay Street Main Level, Toronto, Ontario (tel: 416 968 2220). Plus Montreal

VISITORS WITH DISABILITIES
Plenty of disabled visitors come to Crete, and tour operators will tell you which of their villas or hotels is best equipped for your needs. Most of the major sights can be visited by booking onto excursions and travelling by modern coach. Even so, the rough rocky terrain of archaeological sites means that wheelchair-bound visitors will need help.

ACKNOWLEDGEMENTS

The Automobile Association would like to thank the following photographers, libraries and associations for their assistance in the preparation of this book.
MARY EVANS PICTURE LIBRARY 34, 35a, 35b; HISTORICAL MUSEUM OF CRETE 37; HULTON DEUTSCH COLLECTION LTD 58b, 59; NATURE PHOTOGRAPHERS LTD (B Burbidge) 109, 146, 147b, 148a, 148b; PICTURES COLOUR LIBRARY 64
The remaining photographs are held in the Association's own photo library (AA PHOTO LIBRARY) and were taken by: Philip Enticknap 1, 9, 11, 14, 15a, 15b, 18, 22, 23, 26, 28, 31b, 33, 36, 39, 42/3, 44, 45, 46, 48, 49, 53, 56, 57b, 58a, 61, 63, 77, 80a, 82, 83a, 91, 94/5, 97, 98, 99b, 100a, 100b, 101, 103, 104, 105, 106, 107, 110b, 110c, 111a, 111b, 112, 113, 117c, 123, 127, 144, 147a, 151, 152, 158, 159a, 159b, 160, 172, 173a, 181, 182, 184, 186; Ken Paterson inset, spine, 2, 4, 5, 7, 8, 12, 16, 17, 19, 20, 21, 25, 27, 38, 40, 41, 43, 47, 50, 51, 60, 65, 66, 67, 68a, 68b, 69, 70, 71, 72, 73, 74a, 74b, 75, 76, 78, 79, 80b, 81, 83b, 83c, 84, 85, 87, 89, 99a, 102, 108, 110a, 114, 115, 116, 117a, 117b, 118, 119, 120, 122, 124, 125a, 125b, 126, 128, 129, 131, 133, 135a, 135b, 137, 139a, 139b, 141a, 141b, 142, 143, 145, 149, 150, 153, 154, 155, 156, 157a, 157b, 161, 162, 163, 165, 169, 170, 171, 173b, 174, 175, 176, 177, 185, 187, 189; Wyn Voysey 62, 130, 166
The photographer would like to thank Simply Travel Ltd for their assistance, with special thanks to Chryssa Ninolaki in Crete.

CONTRIBUTORS

Series adviser: Melissa Shales   **Designer:** Design 23   **Copy editor:** Michael Rebane
Verifier: Judy Sykes   **Indexer:** Marie Lorimer